Win

You Got This!!!

MY STRENGTH
IS YOUR STRENGTH

WINNING AGAINST BREAST CANCER
By Valeda Keys

~Valeda

My Strength is Your Strength

Printed in the United States of America

ISBN: 9780692133033

This book is dedicated to my siblings, my nieces, my granddaughter, and my twin sister's granddaughters.

This book is also dedicated to the women that have been recently diagnosed with breast cancer and to the women who have the BRCA2 gene mutation, as well as the caregivers and supporters of this crazy challenge called BREAST CANCER.

Last but not least, to my mother, LaJuanna, my first shero. I love you so much. Your strength is so quiet, yet very strong.

Daddy, Rest On (June 26, 1996).

Thank you to my faithful husband of 16 years, Larry. Thank you for staying and praying. Thank you for being patient and caring, and most importantly for being a God-fearing man. I thank God for showing me the greatness in you, when my life was in crumbles. My God in heaven, thank you so much.

Thank you to my dear friend, Megan for believing in me since the day we met. You have truly had my back. I absolutely love my book cover - it is so "me" and other women. You are the best graphic designer.

Thank you, Vickie for coming to my home to hear my story. You came, you stayed, you listened, you shared — which is really where the publicity started. Thank you for believing in me. I appreciate you.

Thank you to my friend, Amy for asking me, "Is your book finished?" Your voice was always in my mind … "finish the book, Valeda." Thank you for editing my book.

Thank you TT (Arnette) for being the matriarch of the family and one of the best aunts in the entire world. Thank you for being my caregiver after one of the hardest surgeries in my entire life (double mastectomy). Wow!!! I really wouldn't be here if you didn't assist with my recovery from this surgery.

To my aunt Dorothy (Dot), I love you and you too will get through this challenge called breast cancer. Dot is my mother's sister. Aunt Dot was diagnosed with ductal carcinoma in situ (2017) and tested positive for the BRCA2 gene. She received the "My Strength is Your Strength" award at the 6th annual Valeda's Hope Pink and Pearls Luncheon and Conference on Saturday, October 21, 2017.

Thank you to our sons, Eric and Anthony. Cancer wasn't your concern but I knew I had to fight and WIN because of you and give this thing called "LIFE" my best shot.

Thank you Dr. Jovita and Dr. Lannis for taking time out of your busy schedules to read and review my book.

Thank you Dr. Maclin for your input on the Tram Delay chapter and my niece on the Fibroadenoma chapter.

Thank you, LIFE for 'happening.'

MY STRENGTH IS ...  _____

PREFACE

This book serves several purposes. It is an account of
my journey through the ups and downs of breast cancer.
Journaling through the process and telling my story has
been healing and a source of STRENGTH. Sharing it
with others gives me HOPE that my experience can help
others fighting this same battle. The chapters are written
as a memoir, from my own personal experience and are
meant to inform, encourage and inspire. It is not intended
to be a substitute for proper medical advice. I pray that
my story will help make it a little easier for someone else
to fight and WIN.

My Strength Is Your Strength.

MY STRENGTH IS ... _____

1 | DREAM

dream: a series of thoughts, images, and sensations occurring in a person's mind during sleep

I normally don't have dreams but when I do have a dream and I remember it there is something true to the dream. I had a dream when I was 34 years old that I would deal with the challenge of breast cancer. Notice, I said, "challenge." I woke up and called my mother and told her about the dream and she said to me, "I wouldn't believe that dream." In my heart I felt like this was something that I would have to go through to help other women. In the dream God spoke to me and said, "Treat this cancer like a common cold because you will get over it."

My Strength Is Your Strength.

MY STRENGTH IS ... _____

2 | IT'S OKAY TO TAKE A NAP

My mother used to make us take naps all the time as kids. Napping was definitely part of my childhood. I still take naps. It's a must in my life. I personally believe that napping was a part of my healing during this journey through breast cancer. Taking a nap, to me, is a form of meditation. I call it a "mental recovery." We definitely shouldn't feel bad about taking naps.

NOW, DON'T THINK ABOUT TAKING A NAP ... FINISH THE BOOK!

Here are some reasons why naps are good:

1. A nap restores alertness. You know how your energy depletes in the early afternoon? You start feeling a little sleepy and lose focus. It happens to most of us. A quick nap brings us back to reality. The National Sleep Foundation (http://www.sleepfoundation.org/article/sleep-topics/napping) recommends a short nap of twenty to thirty minutes for improved alertness and performance, without leaving you feeling groggy or interfering with nighttime sleep.

2. A nap prevents burnout. We are not meant to race and not rest. We are always busy. Step back and take a nap.
3. A nap increases sensory perception. According to Dr. Sara C. Nednick, author of *Take A Nap, Change Your Life*, napping can restore the sensitivity of sight, hearing and taste.
4. A nap reduces the risk of heart disease. Did you know those who take a midday siesta at least three times a week are 37 percent less likely to die of heart disease? Working men are 64 percent less likely. It's true according to a 2007 study published in the Archives of Internal Medicine.

Napping Celebrities:
- Eleanor Roosevelt, the wife of President Franklin D. Roosevelt, used to boost her energy by napping before speaking engagements.
- Though criticized for it, President Ronald Reagan famously took naps as well.
- Physicist Albert Einstein napped each day — on top of getting ten hours of sleep each night.
- President John F. Kennedy ate his lunch in bed and then settled in for a nap — everyday!
- Oil industrialist and philanthropist John D. Rockefeller napped every day in his office.

I WILL ALWAYS TAKE A NAP. IT'S GOOD FOR ME ... AND YOU.

My Strength Is Your Strength.

3 | DA VINCI SURGERY — YES, HYSTERECTOMY

The da Vinci Surgical System is a robotic surgical system
made by the American company, Intuitive Surgical.
Sometimes it's called "The Robot Surgery," which is
good because sometimes I forget the word da Vinci. My
breast surgeon, Dr. Diane Radford recommended that my
family members and I have this surgery due to us having
the BRCA2 gene mutation.

Having the BRCA2 gene mutation means you are at risk
for having breast and ovarian cancer as well. The main
questions asked before having this surgery are: Do you
plan on having children? Do you plan to have any more
children? Are you finished having children?

First and foremost, I highly recommend this surgery if
you're considering a hysterectomy. Why you ask?
Here's why ...
   • Shortened hospital stay
   • Less blood loss
   • Fewer complications, including less risk of
     infection
   • Faster return to normal activities
   • Less pain

My family members have considered prophylactic surgeries due to my journey.

I personally love not having to go buy maxi pads (I never did like tampons) and not having a monthly menstrual cycle is GREAT. I started my period when I was 11 years old. That's long enough, ladybug.

The benefits of a hysterectomy for me:
- No period
- No pads
- No cramps
- Sex anytime I want with my husband

Disadvantages of a hysterectomy for me (I have to be honest):
- Hot flashes! One minute you are cold, then the next minute you are hot. Solution ... keep a mini fan with you at your office and while on vacations.
- Weight gain and hunger. Realize why you are eating and what you are eating. Solution ... exercise must become a lifestyle.

"According to the Centers for Disease Control and Prevention (CDC), from 2006-2010, 11.7 percent of women between the ages of 40-44 had a hysterectomy. Approximately 600,000 hysterectomies are performed annually in the United States, and approximately 20 million Americans have had a hysterectomy."

Uterine prolapse, which is a sliding of the uterus from its normal position into the vaginal canal, is another reason for hysterectomy.

Are you in need of a hysterectomy? Have a lot of women in your family had hysterectomies? Do you have uterine fibroids that cause pain, bleeding or other problems? Was this information helpful? Are you afraid? If so ...

My Strength Is Your Strength

MY STRENGTH IS ... _____

4 | TAMOXIFEN

I started taking Tamoxifen on August 6, 2010, my mother's birthday. I started taking Tamoxifen on this particular day and wanted to remember the stop date which would have been August 6, 2015, exactly five years later.

I took Tamoxifen every day without fail like it was a vitamin until I had to stop on August 11, 2011.

Tamoxifen, the generic name for Nolvadex, is approved by the U.S. Food and Drug Administration (FDA) to treat women and men diagnosed with hormone-receptor-positive and early-stage breast cancer after surgery (or possibly chemotherapy and radiation) to reduce the changes of the cancer coming back (recurring).

Tamoxifen made me gain weight. I was always hungry, even in my sleep, LOL! And, it also made me have really bad joint pain.

I am not a doctor, but I personally and honestly wouldn't recommend this medication if you have the BRCA2 gene

mutation. Tamoxifen is not an expensive drug at all, but still, I feel, it was just a waste of money for me.

My Strength Is Your Strength

5 | BRCA2

The **BRCA** test is a blood test to check for specific changes (mutations) in genes that help control normal cell growth. Finding changes in these genes, called BRCA1 and BRCA2, can help determine your chance of developing breast, ovarian, and other cancers like prostate and pancreatic.

Yes, my family has this gene.

Genetic counselors are helpful in determining what type of testing is best and it is usually covered by insurance if certain criterias are met. There are different types of BRCA testing, ranging in cost from $475 to about $4,000. Testing is less expensive once a mutation has been identified within a family and thanks to my insurance, I don't remember having to pay anything for mine. Also keep in mind, it takes 5-7 days to get the test results back.

So, basically BRCA1 and BRCA2 are the genes linked to breast cancer, ovarian, and cervical cancer. I highly recommend this testing if your mother, sister, aunt or

MYRIAD

PATIENT COPY
Comprehensive BRACAnalysis®
BRCA1 and BRCA2 Analysis Result

SPECIMEN		PATIENT	
Specimen Type	Blood	Name	Keys, Valeda
Draw Date:	May 05, 2010	Date of Birth	E1302566520
Accession Date	May 07, 2010	Patient ID:	Female
Report Date	May 17, 2010	Gender:	00570285-BLD
		Accession #	1704561
		Requisition #	

PHYSICIAN
Diane Radford, MD
St Louis Cancer and Breast Institute
450 N New Ballas
Suite 270 W
St Louis, MO 53141

Test Results and Interpretation

POSITIVE FOR A DELETERIOUS MUTATION

Result	Interpretation
No Mutation Detected	No Mutation Detected
No Mutation Detected	No Mutation Detected
5844del5	Deleterious

Test Performed
BRCA1 sequencing
5-site rearrangement panel

BRCA2 sequencing

Analysis consists of sequencing of all translated exons and immediately adjacent intronic regions of the BRCA1 and BRCA2 genes, test for five specific BRCA1 rearrangements. The classification and interpretation of all variants identified in this assay reflects the state of scientific understanding at the time this report was issued. In some instances, the classification and interpretation of such may change as new scientific information becomes available.

The results of this analysis are consistent with the germline BRCA2 mutation 5844del5, resulting in premature truncation of the B protein at amino acid position 1873. Although the exact risk of breast and ovarian cancer conferred by this specific mutation has determined, studies of this type of mutation in high-risk families indicate that deleterious mutations in BRCA2 may confer as mu an 84% risk of breast cancer and a 27% risk of ovarian cancer by age 70 in women within five years of the first (J Clin Oncol 17:139 in BRCA2 have been reported to confer a 12% risk of a second breast cancer (J Natl Cancer Inst 91:1310-1315, 1999). This mutation may also 1998), as well as a 16% risk of subsequent ovarian cancer (J Natl Cancer Inst 91:1310-1315, 199 a 6% risk of male breast cancer by age 70 and 20% risk of prostate cancer by age 80 (J Natl Cancer Inst 91:1310-1315, 199 as increased (albeit low) risks of some other cancers. Each first degree relative of this individual has a one-in-two chance of mutation. Family members can be tested for this specific mutation with a single site analysis

Please contact Myriad Professional Support at 1-800-469-7423 to discuss any questions regarding this

Report ...

YOUR
STRENGTH.

Positive for a Deleterious Mutation or Suspected Deleterious

Dear_____,

I recently had genetic testing to help me understand my risk of developing cancer. I was tested for inherited changes or mutations in the BRCA1 and BRCA2 genes. Mutations in these genes cause most cases of hereditary breast and ovarian cancer. My test identified a mutation that runs in our family. The specific mutation is listed on a copy of my test results, which I have enclosed with this letter.

This test result means I have hereditary breast and ovarian cancer syndrome. This syndrome significantly increased my risk of breast and ovarian cancer. Fortunately, there are medical options to reduce my risks, which is why knowing about a mutation will be very helpful.

It is possible that other people in our family also have this mutation. I am writing to all the relatives on the side of our family that has the cancer history. You may want to talk to your doctor about whether genetic testing makes sense for you. As I mentioned, I have included a copy of my test result with this letter to help if you decide to get more information. These results will help you and your doctor manage your cancer risk.

You can also contact Myriad Genetic Laboratories (the laboratory that did my testing) to get more information or to find a doctor who is familiar with BRACAnalysis testing call 1-800-469-7423 or go to www.myriadtests.com. I hope you find this information helpful. Please let me know if you have any questions for me.

Sincerely,

Valeda Keys

grandmother has had breast cancer or cervical cancer.

My mother didn't want to have this testing done for herself until I was diagnosed for the *second* time. I thank God she finally did!

Do you think you or anyone in your family needs to have this test? Don't be afraid. It's better to know than not to know.

My Strength Is Your Strength

6 | FRIDAY, APRIL 2, 2010

It was Good Friday, I was off work and able to get my mammogram.

My Strength Is Your Strength

MY STRENGTH IS ... _____

7 | WHAT IS A MAMMOGRAM?

A mammogram is an x-ray picture of the breast. Doctors use a mammogram to look for early signs of breast cancer. Regular mammograms are the best tests doctors have to find breast cancer early, sometimes up to three years before it can be felt.

To put it into perspective, I'd rather have a mammogram than a well-woman exam (pap smear) or teeth cleaning. Now don't get me wrong, they all are very important. A mammogram is not painful, it's just uncomfortable. That's my opinion.

I no longer have to have mammograms. However, if you are a woman and 40 years of age, you need a mammogram annually. Mammograms don't prevent breast cancer but mammography is the most effective screening tool used today to find breast cancer in most women. Mammograms are available free of charge if you don't have medical insurance. My mammograms started at the age of 27 and ended at the of age 39.

My Strength Is Your Strength

MY STRENGTH IS ... _____

8 | MAMMOGRAMS WITH MRI FOLLOW-UP

After my first cancer, it was recommended that I have
mammograms every six months. A mammogram with
MRI follow-up found my second cancer. MRI is used
in women who already have been diagnosed with breast
cancer, to help measure the size of the cancer, to look for
other tumors in the breast, and to check for tumors in the
opposite breast.

For women that are at high-risk for getting breast
cancer, a screening MRI is recommended along with a
yearly mammogram. An MRI is not recommended as a
screening test by itself because it can miss some cancers
that a mammogram can find. The MRI scan takes pictures
from many angles. One of the main things I remember
about this is you are in an enclosed space for a long
amount of time — usually 45 to 60 minutes. That's a
shame — Jesus, Joseph and Mary! I would recommend
asking your doctor for something to keep you calm
during the test. You have to lie face down on a narrow flat
table. Your breasts will hang down into a opening in the
table so they can be scanned without being compressed.

Know your allergies too. Make sure you tell them if you have any metal objects in your body. I had titanium in the left breast where the cancer was located from the first diagnosis for radiation administration. The process of having an MRI is exhausting, but not painful.

My Strength Is Your Strength

9 | STEREOTACTIC BREAST BIOPSY

This is a procedure that identifies that you really do have breast cancer. It is done because the radiologist sees something wrong on your mammogram that can't be felt. It is called stereotactic because it utilizes two images taken of the same location from slightly different angles.

My core biopsy from the left breast revealed a ductal carcinoma in situ (DCIS). The in situ carcinoma exhibits high-grade cytology and a solid architectural pattern with comedo necrosis and associated calcifications (this is what my pathology report said).

After this procedure, my left breast was bruised pretty badly — it turned purple in color. You are lying on your stomach for up to an hour for this procedure. After which, I was given a cold pack to help with pain and inflammation. I was able to return to work the next day and just took Ibuprofen for the pain. I thought to myself, "This bruising looks really bad. Is this what breast cancer look like?" I remember seeing blood splattered while the procedure was being done. Afterwards, pressure is applied to prevent bleeding and then a bandage is applied to keep the area closed and to prevent infection. A small

metal clip is left in place where the biopsy was done, so it can easily be located during surgery, radiation, and future mammograms.

You should contact your doctor if you develop fever, redness, warmth, or notice discharge from the site. These are all signs of infection.

What is cytology?
Cytology is the study of microscopic appearance of cells, especially for the diagnosis of abnormalities and malignancies.

What is comedo necrosis?
Comedo carcinoma of the breast is actually a type of ductal carcinoma in situ. It is characterized by the presence of central necrosis, or evidence of cell death and decay. However, comedo carcinoma is considered to be of a higher grade and a little more aggressive than others and may be treated a little more aggressively.

What are calcifications?
These are calcium deposits that develop in a woman's breast tissue. They are very common and are usually benign (non-cancerous). In some instances, certain types of breast calcifications may suggest early breast cancer.

Remember, you can ask your doctor for something to keep you calm during and before procedure. Don't be afraid to ask your doctor for your results and records for every test. Keep everything in one place. You've only got one body and we have to take care of it and know what the doctors are saying about it. My biopsy was done Thursday, April 22, 2010.

My Strength Is Your Strength

STRENGTH IS ... _____

10 | APRIL 26, 2010

I was 37 years old, in school, taking prerequisites to become a registered nurse and working Monday through Friday as a nurse at St. Louis Job Corps Center. It was a Thursday evening and I was very tired. It was 5:26 p.m. I received a phone call from a breast surgeon (but not *my* breast surgeon). The doctor asked me, "May I speak with Valeda Keys?"

I said, "This is she."

"Valeda, you have ductal carcinoma in situ and call our office in the morning to discuss further."

I thought to myself, "What a way to give a diagnosis — over the phone? Really? Wow!!!"

My mother said this is how it happened for her too. I think this is the most ridiculous thing to do to a person … to give them bad news over the phone. Luckily, I am a nurse and knew what ductal in situ meant. Some women don't have a clue when they receive that diagnosis over the phone. What if I had already been discouraged about something or already in a crisis? It should not be this way.

I called it an "interruption of life." I was actually in the middle of starting dinner. Both of my sons were at home, so I told them. I hadn't really seen my sons cry since they were babies ... not like that anyway. Anthony was only 12 years old, about to turn 13 on May 19, 2010. My oldest son, Eric (19) was home from college that day. I called my husband on his cell phone ... he hadn't made it home from work yet. His response on the phone was, "We will get through this." After that I texted some family and friends. I said to them, "I have breast cancer but I will live." A few friends came by and my Aunt T. T. came over. My mother was at work but she knew if my aunt was there I would be okay.

My Strength Is Your Strength

11 | LUMPECTOMY

This was surgery #1. Thursday, May 13, 2010 ... six days before our youngest son's 13th birthday. I just wanted the cancer out.

Lumpectomy: a surgical removal of a discrete portion or "lump" of breast tissue usually in the treatment of a malignant tumor or breast cancer

I wasn't allowed to take aspirin or any aspirin products a week before surgery because it can cause increased bleeding during surgery. You are allowed to take your heart and blood pressure medication the morning of surgery (with a sip of water). I believe this is to keep your blood pressure stable during surgery.

My surgery was done at the St. Louis Surgical Center. It was a same-day surgery. I was given Percocet for the pain and learned that I was allergic to it. I started itching really badly, and I remember talking to my twin who told me she was allergic to Percocet too. I called Dr. Radford and she told me to stop taking it and to take some Benadryl to stop the itching. After this surgery you follow up

with your breast surgeon in a week unless you face any challenges.

When I arrived home from the surgery my sister brought me some Lee's chicken. It was so good, probably because I couldn't eat anything after midnight to prep for my surgery, so I was hungry. I came home with bandages that you are allowed to remove after 24 hours, according to my post-operative instruction form. I didn't have any scars after this surgery. You are allowed to take a shower in 24 hours however, Steri strips are to stay in place until the strips fall off by themselves.

I tried to keep all my medical forms and information. You can always ask for your medical records. I knew I would write a book someday, that's why I tried to keep as much information as possible.

Even though this is a same-day surgery, you will need someone to drive you to your surgery, or your surgery will be cancelled.

After surgery, there is still some anxiety present which is why I was given a prescription for Xanax (1 tablet every six hours as needed for anxiety). Sometimes you do need something to keep you calm. You can't be afraid to inform your physician of how you're doing and how you're feeling ... both physically and emotionally.

You have to wait for at least a week for your surgeon to

call you to give you your pathology results. Dr. Radford called me a week later and said, "Valeda, all margins are clear." All I knew was that sounded positive and that's what you want to hear.

At the end of the day, this surgery was not complicated and the pain afterwards was tolerable.

My Strength Is Your Strength

MY STRENGTH IS ... _____

12 | DUCTAL CARCINOMA IN SITU (DCIS)

Ductal carcinoma in situ is the most common type of non-invasive breast cancer. It's a pre-cancerous lesion. Ductal means that the cancer starts inside the milk ducts. Carcinoma refers to any cancer that begins in the skin or other tissues (including breast tissue) that covers or lines the internal organs. And, in situ means "in its original place." DCIS is called "non-invasive" because it hasn't spread beyond the milk duct into any normal surrounding breast tissue. DCIS isn't life-threatening, but having DCIS can increase the risk of developing an invasive breast cancer later on. When you have had DCIS, you are at higher risk for the cancer coming back or for developing a new breast cancer than a person who has never had breast cancer before.

My Strength Is Your Strength

MY STRENGTH IS ... _____

13 | RADIATION THERAPY

I received radiation after my lumpectomy, which was recommended by my doctor. There are three main things that are very important to know about radiation.

1. Do not wear deodorant. If you have to wear deodorant please wear Tom's.
2. You can't move while getting radiation, so plan to sit still while getting your treatments. This can be annoying, especially if your back or scalp starts to itch while getting treatments.
3. Infection can happen because your skin becomes very sensitive. In fact, your skin begins to peel after so many treatments and it has a pretty bad appearance but the good thing is your skin comes back ... it's just not the same. Unfortunately, I did get an infection during radiation treatments.

Nothing is the same after cancer. I received 33 treatments of radiation. Seven weeks of doing the same thing daily. Radiation was Monday through Friday. The doctors suggested that I rest on the weekends. The treatments are no longer than 30 to 40 minutes, sometimes even a

shorter length of time. I started radiation on June 7, 2010 and I ended on July 23, 2010. I also had my 38th birthday while receiving treatments. It was June 18 — on a Friday.

Radiation treatments were done at The David C. Pratt Center. I would leave work each day an hour early to get to my appointment on time. You can still work and drive yourself to your treatments. If I had to do this all over again, I wouldn't work during treatments. Your body is under a lot of stress and you don't even realize it. I would definitely suggest, if you don't have to work while getting treatments, please don't.

You no longer should be wearing bras with underwire. I wore white cotton sports bras after the infection occurred. Whether you are receiving radiation on your right breast or left breast, you must treat this area with care. It is now your baby!! No lotions or perfumes should be on this area.

Radiation therapy can be delivered externally or internally. External radiation delivers high-energy rays to the cancer from a machine outside the body. External Beam Radiation Therapy (EBRT) is given via machines called linear accelerators, which produce high-energy external radiation beams that penetrate the tissues and deliver the radiation dose deep in the areas where the cancer resides. ERBT is typically delivered on an outpatient basis for approximately 6 to 8 weeks. It begins with a planning session, or simulation, during which the radiation oncologist places marks on the body and takes measurements in order to line up the radiation beam in the correct position for each treatment. During treatment, you are lying on a table and treated with radiation from multiple directions. The actual area receiving radiation treatment may be large or small, depending on the cancer. Radiation can be delivered specifically to an organ or encompass the surrounding area, including the lymph nodes.

My Strength Is Your Strength

MY
STRENGTH IS ...  _____

14 | SHINGLES

Yes, having shingles was part of my breast cancer
journey in October of 2010, due to a compromised
immune system from the radiation treatments.

**Shingles: a disease caused by the varicella-zoster
virus, especially by reactivated virus in an older
person, characterized by skin eruptions and pain
along the course of involved sensory nerves**

It is very painful and contagious.

At first, the doctors thought it was a spider bite. I went to
urgent care and took the medication that was prescribed,
but it wasn't working. The pain had gotten so bad I
couldn't even say my name. I went to the hospital closest
to my home, DePaul Hospital. A physician immediately
diagnosed me after reading my recent medical history.
She had experienced shingles too after her radiation
treatments from a breast cancer diagnosis, so she knew
exactly what it was.

The shingles were located on the left side of my forehead,

a blister with a fluid-filled appearance. The physician told me that due to the location, the shingles could cause hospitalization or even blindness. I remember praying immediately, "Lord, please don't let me be hospitalized or go blind, let these shingles stay right here." God answered my prayer — it did not spread. Everything happens according to your FAITH.

At this time, I was in an accelerated RN school, doing my clinicals at Lutheran School of Nursing. The medication I was prescribed for my shingles was a large turquoise bluish tablet called **Valtrex**. Very hard to swallow!

My shingles lasted about two weeks. Remember, this is contagious and you definitely can't be around pregnant women. So, not only did I have to withdraw from school, I had to take off work as well because I was exposed to young women who were pregnant.

There is no cure for shingles but treatment may shorten the length of illness and prevent complications. Treatment options include antiviral medicines to reduce the pain and duration of symptoms.

My Strength Is Your Strength

15 | THURSDAY, AUGUST 11, 2011

This is a day that will never be forgotten.

I wasn't at work for even two hours when I received a phone call at 8:30 a.m. from my medical oncologist. While I was still employed at St. Louis Job Corps, I was getting a chart for a student, when my cell phone rang and woman on the other end said, "Valeda, this is Dr. Susan Luedke. You have breast cancer again! Can you come to my office at 3 p.m. to discuss your options?"

I really didn't know how I was going to make it through my day. I ran to the back of the office. I started hyperventilating and screaming. All I wanted was my bed and my mama. I was so mad, I mean so, so, so mad. I knew I had a BIG FIGHT ahead of me and a long one. I finally kinda stopped crying, with the help of my co-workers consoling me and I called my husband. He said, "We will get through this again." I stayed at work until 2:00 p.m. I wanted to leave work sooner but I had no paid time off and couldn't afford to take time off because I knew I was going to need some days for my treatment.

My husband met me at home and we went to see my medical oncologist. This day was so long and I couldn't wait for it to be over. My aunt also met us there at the oncologist office. Upon arrival, Dr. Luedke got us right in — no waiting. Dr. Luedke said to me, "Honey, you have breast cancer again and it's not playing well with your body. If you don't get both breasts removed, you are looking at a third cancer — especially with this gene. Go home and throw the Tamoxifen away. It didn't work for you."

I really was at a loss for words and I knew I had to do this for myself. I just wasn't ready to lose my breasts. My mind wasn't ready for this, but I knew I had to mentally prepare.

As we drove home I saw tears running down my husband's face. I remember telling him, "Darnell (I like to call him by his middle name), this is too much for me and if you would like to go on with your life, you can, because this is too much for me to handle."

He was at a loss for words too, you could tell. It was a long drive home. From this day forward I remember just being on my knees at night praying for strength and ways to get through this ... mentally first. Everything starts in the mind. God gave me a scripture to stand on — Psalm 118:17 KJV (King James Version) Bible. "I shall not die but live, and will declare the works of the Lord."

I believe the first two things that came to mind after being diagnosed with breast cancer were DEATH and PAIN. You have to find STRENGTH and HOPE to survive and win.

My Strength Is Your Strength

STRENGTH IS ... _____

16 | DOUBLE MASTECTOMY (SURGERY #3)

What is a double mastectomy?
A double mastectomy is the removal of both breasts.
This can be done by removing all skin and breast tissue,
and leaving the chest wall flat, or by removing the breast
tissue, while leaving the nipple and areola, and the skin
of the breast. A plastic surgeon can come in at the same
surgery and do immediate reconstruction of the breast.
One of the most common reasons that a woman has a
double mastectomy is when she is found to be carrying
a gene mutation that gives a very high lifetime risk of
breast cancer.

I truly wanted my breasts, but I couldn't have them. Out
of all my surgeries this one was one the worst. The most
ridiculous thing about this surgery is that after a woman
has this major surgery, she is discharged within 24 hours.
This is insane! I hope this changes in the future because
being discharged just 24 hours after such a major surgery
is crazy.

I had my surgery on September 12, 2011. I can't lie, just
the thought of not having the breasts you were born with
is a really scary experience. It was my niece's birthday. I

would have changed the surgery date if I had been in my right mind, but I just didn't think about it at the time.

I believe I was in surgery for 3 to 5 hours and discharged from the hospital the next day. I remember telling my doctors Dr. Diane Radford, my breast surgeon, and Dr. Melvin Maclin, my plastic surgeon, "When I wake up from surgery I don't want to wake up flat-chested." I was a 44DD!! I just couldn't imagine waking up every day being flat-chested. Some women can ... and do ... and they are okay with that. It's definitely a mind thing ... I liked my breasts and I didn't want to see them taken away by cancer.

My husband wanted me to be looked after while he was at work and our sons were at school so I stayed with my aunt for about two weeks. I was extremely weak and nauseated when I arrived at her house. All I wanted was a bed. I remember thinking, "Why would they discharge me? I hoped and prayed I made it through the night. Vicodin was one of the medications prescribed. Vicodin made me constipated after a while, so it is very important to drink plenty of water and eat plenty of fiber after this surgery. Eat your favorite fiber foods if you have to take Vicodin and you want to prevent being constipated. Cantaloupe was a good source of fiber for me.

So, back to the notion that I didn't want to be flat-chested after surgery. I didn't come home flat-chested. I came home with what you call tissue expanders.
Tissue Expansion: a common breast reconstruction

technique, which involves expansion of the breast skin and muscle using a temporary tissue expander. A few months later, the expander is removed and the patient receives either microvascular flap reconstruction, or the insertion of a permanent breast implant.

Just for the record, my tissue expanders (aka turtle shells) stayed in from September, 2011 until March, 2013. I had to lose weight for the TRAM surgery and also had to have a hysterectomy due to the BRCA gene ... Complicated ... Complicated. At the time of this surgery I was overweight, 200 plus pounds and I would consider myself unhealthy because I didn't exercise regularly. I was 39 years old.

When you have tissue expanders you will go see your plastic surgeon to get fills. Fills are when salt water is injected into the expander every two to three weeks for about three to four months. This is done until the chest skin has stretched to the desired size. The expander is usually removed and replaced by an implant. Some expanders can be kept in place like an implant. That's how it was for me. My breasts were lopsided because I had radiation from my previous cancer and the breast could only stretch so much ... my skin had already been through enough. The left breast was the one that was lopsided. It was pretty noticeable if I wore the wrong blouse but it could only take so many salt water fills before it wasn't able to stretch anymore.

Those expansion fills are uncomfortable as well. I would

recommend taking Ibuprofen before your appointment.
I was referred to Medical West Breast Prosthesis Center
to get a prosthesis for the lopsidedness. Initially, when I
walked in I was of course, discouraged and disappointed
because I had to walk through another store to get to
the breast prosthesis center. The woman I was working
with, she was so supportive. I went by myself, which was
probably a bad idea. I was so emotional. The woman told
me, "You are at the beginning stages of this process, you
will become better with time. I had a double mastectomy
too, years ago." She then gave me some Kleenex to wipe
away the tears. She started measuring me and getting
me fitted for the prosthesis due to the lopsidedness. She
even showed me her breasts, which I thought to myself,
"Wow!!! And, Thank You" ... I needed to see that
because I was still in the "I don't know stage." I ended
up walking out of there with two bras paid for by our
insurance company.

Women's Health and Cancer Rights Act, or WHCRA,
is a federal law that was passed in 1998 in order to
provide certain protections and coverage to patients who
choose to have breast reconstruction surgery following a
mastectomy. The Women's Health and Cancer Rights Act
requires ALL group health plans that cover mastectomies
to also provide coverage for reconstructive surgery, as
well as other post-mastectomy benefits. The WHCRA
covers women who undergo a mastectomy for any
medical reason, not just to treat breast cancer.

When immediate reconstruction is performed, studies have shown that it is psychologically beneficial to the woman. I find this to be so true. I personally couldn't imagine coming home flat-chested. But, I believe your decisions are based off your age, spousal-opinion, and where you are in life at the time of your mastectomy. I have noticed that many older women opt for just wearing a prosthesis for the rest of their life. Older women tend not to want to go through all the extra surgeries which, after having gone through them myself, I really can't blame them. Of course, at the end of the day, reconstruction is a personal choice, and every woman makes a choice based on her own personal feelings.

Wearing blazers became very common for me during this transition. I found myself buying blazers and light jackets and wearing them daily because I was still self-conscious, even after wearing the prosthesis. Plus, you could still tell if you looked close enough. Every woman has a blue jean jacket, and my blue jean jacket became one of my favorite daily wears. Really it was all in my mind and my own self-consciousness. One other thing that made me feel better was wearing a SPORTS BRA. This made me feel so comfortable. It was something about wearing a sports bra versus a regular bra that comforted me. My skin on the left side/left breast area was very sensitive again, and the tissue expanders were very uncomfortable. I also wouldn't recommend anything with underwire. So, for me, I just found a sports bra to be better than anything for support and comfort during this period.

YOU DO WHAT WORKS FOR YOU DURING THIS TIME.

My Strength Is Your Strength

17 | THEM DAMN DRAINS, UGH

When you have a double mastectomy, your surgeon will often place surgical drains at your mastectomy site and one in your armpit if you have lymph nodes removed to help speed up your healing. These surgical drains may be called grenade drains, Jackson-Pratt drains, or JP drains. You will have a drainage tube and a drainage bulb outside your skin near your surgical incision. Part of the drainage tube will be inside your body into the surgical area, where it will collect blood and lymphatic fluid. The drainage tube will be held in place with a suture, so that it doesn't accidentally slip out.

The drains are used to measure the fluid daily, and keep a record of how much blood and lymphatic fluid is removed. As the volume of fluid decreases, swelling around your surgical site should also decrease. When the fluid volume is 30mL or less in a 24-hour period, you can have the drains removed. I had 3 drains for this surgery. These drains help prevent hematomas and lymphedema from occurring. I have to admit, the drains are very uncomfortable as well. They are like your babies while

recovering and require gentle care to keep the area clean and free from infection. While your drains are in, you want to make things as easy as possible for yourself. I would highly recommend wearing a button-down gown because you can easily get to them for recording the fluids and it's just less complicated. During this time it's hard to raise your hands above your head. I would also recommend wearing a button-down shirt when going to the doctor while you have the drains. I wore the same few shirts – you can wear your spouse's shirts or go to a local resale shop and buy a few.

My Strength Is Your Strength

18 | PHYSICAL THERAPY

Physical therapy (PT) after a double mastectomy is a hidden blessing. After my double mastectomy, I literally couldn't lift my hands over my head. I knew I couldn't live like this for the rest of my life. Sometimes the doctor may not offer PT to you. Just ask!!! It's your body and doctors won't know exactly how you are feeling. Just ask, "Can you please arrange for me to have some physical therapy for my upper body strength?" This is usually no problem. You can ask your breast surgeon or your plastic surgeon. Of course, your medical insurance will play a big part. My physical therapy was done at DePaul Health Center. You usually have the option to go where you choose. I chose somewhere close to home.

Physical therapy is a form of healing, and getting the right therapist is important. Food for thought: BE KIND to all the people that are taking care of you. It is important for you and your body. On the other hand, if you feel uncomfortable with the physical therapist you are assigned to, don't hesitate to seek a new one. You should never feel uncomfortable. Some of the exercises

may make you feel uncomfortable but you shouldn't ever personally feel uncomfortable. My physical therapist was a male and he made me feel comfortable not uncomfortable. If you know you won't be comfortable with a male physical therapist, ask for a female before you even begin going. Be good to your body and to others.

Physical therapists (PTs) are highly-educated, licensed healthcare professionals who can help patients reduce pain and improve or restore mobility – in many cases without expensive surgery and often reducing the need for long-term use of prescription medications and their side effects.

Three Classic Strength Training Exercises For Arms After A Double Mastectomy

*** Always consult with your physician first. ***

Start with one set of 10 repetitions for each exercise and add reps and weight as you get stronger and begin to rebuild muscle:

1. **Biceps Curl:** Sit with your arm extended on a table or counter at shoulder height, holding the weight in your hand bend your elbow, bringing your hand toward your shoulder, then straighten your arm back to the starting position. Repeat with the other arm.
2. **Triceps Extension:** Lie on your back with your knees bent, feet flat on the floor, holding the weight in your

hand. Bend your elbow to 90 degrees then straighten your arm back to start. Repeat with the other arm.

3. **Deltoid Raise:** Sit or stand with your arms by your side, palms facing in, holding a weight in each hand; raise both arms out to the sides to shoulder level, then lower back to start. Be sure to keep your arms straight but not stiff.

My Strength Is Your Strength

MY STRENGTH IS ...

19 | MY SEX LIFE AFTER THEY ARE GONE!!!!!

Let's just say this, my sex life is still the same (great). We must not look at what we have lost but look at what we have left. Use your imagination.

Marriage should be honored by all, and the marriage bed kept pure, for God will judge the adulterer and all the sexually immoral. Hebrews 13:4.

Nothing has really changed in my sex life except that I just lost the breasts that I was born with. The breasts that I have now ... they are not part of our sex life. I have to be honest, "I wish they were." My breasts were totally part of my sex life before my cancer, but now unfortunately, post-cancer, they are not. I have gotten a lot of questions from women about this subject so that's why I chose to be open about the subject.

My recommendations:

1. Take a picture of your breasts before you have a double mastectomy.

2. If your breasts are a part of your sex life, "use them before you lose them." The night before surgery is a good time, and the last time, so "go for it." Once your breasts are gone, they are gone. I am still looking for mine (joking). To date, my new breasts are not a part of my sex life. "Why," you ask? Well, because after a double mastectomy, you have little to no feeling. Let me clarify ... you do have some feeling but not the same feeling you had before surgery. I personally think my husband doesn't have a desire to touch them after all we've been through. I mean he has touched them but I can't really feel anything ... I just know his hand is there. Really everything is perfectly understandable. When you have cancer, your husband or mate has cancer too ... they just don't have it physically. They have cancer mentally and socially, especially if they truly love you. Remember to pray for your spouse, as well as yourself, while you are going through this challenge

3. Remember to continue to have sex! Love your husband, wife or mate for staying and praying.

My Strength Is Your Strength

20 | MY GIFT FROM GOD

There was a reason God told me that my husband was
"his gift to me from Him." For that I say, "Thank you,
Lord." My husband never missed a surgery. He never
looked at me in disgust. He supported every decision I
had to make during this time of my life. We had been
married seven years when I was first diagnosed.

I met my husband at one of the jobs I worked at as
a nurse. I remember being in an interview for this
particular job. The interview was an extremely long
one. I was 28 years old. During this particular interview,
the Lord spoke to me and said, "Your husband is here."
I didn't have a clue who it could've been. I dated
my future husband for two years. We did premarital
counseling. Premarital counseling is good but it doesn't
really prepare you for the bumps and bruises that will
happen. I married my husband on September 14, 2002
at 2:30 p.m. at The City Of Life Christian Church,
University City, Missouri. I was 30 years old and he was
37. My husband and I don't have any children together
but he has been a father indeed to our sons.

During the time of my breast cancer, my husband has changed my dressings, given me baths, slept alone, endured overnight stays at the hospital, cried after my second diagnosis, and cooked and cleaned without complaining. He honestly does all the cleaning anyway. My cleaning is not as good as his. He is a perfectionist. You can eat off our garage floor. Seriously. You want to know the truth about it, my husband has even had to clean me up after a bowel movement after my double mastectomy. I know this is probably too much information but this is true information that you may or may not have to go through with your spouse. After my double mastectomy I couldn't reach back there so my husband had to assist. Let me just say, "You really know who you married when these trials come." These trials can make or break a marriage. My husband **PRAYED AND STAYED**.

Larry is from Mississippi. He was raised by his grandparents. I love my husband and I am very grateful for him and his patience. I can be 'something else' at times. During this journey, I would sometimes feel sorry for myself. My husband would be the one who would give me an encouraging word. He would pray with me and when I couldn't pray for myself he would pray for me. It is very important to be married to a God-fearing, praying husband. It takes a strong man to stand by his woman after being diagnosed twice with breast cancer, then to have both of her breasts removed. I even told him at one point, "Leave and enjoy your life because this is

too much for me, so I know it's gotta be too much for you."
He said, "We are in this together, it's not your fault, it's
something you inherited, I'm here to stick it out with you."

Many of you may or may not believe in horoscopes …
but I do. My husband is an Aquarius and I am a Gemini.
We are so compatible. Thank God! Larry loves to wash
cars and landscape. He also loves sports. He loves ESPN.
He respects LeBron James. We've been to a couple of his
games. We don't have a perfect marriage or even the best
marriage but we definitely don't have the worst marriage.
Our home is peaceful. We work as a team. We date. We
say, "I love you." We complement each other. We have
more GOOD days than BAD days. We respect and trust
each other. We believe in each other. We know each
other's strengths and weaknesses. I know when to be
quiet and when to speak. It will be 17 years of marriage
this September. I feel like we are just getting started.

My Strength Is Your Strength

MY STRENGTH IS ... _____

21 | DADDY

My father was born on January 12, 1948. He would be 71 right now. He died at the age of 46 … heart failure was the cause. At the age of 44, he was given 24 months to live. My father didn't want to get on the waiting list for a heart transplant until it was too late. My father did get a pacemaker and a defibrillator, but neither worked. My father was a well-groomed man. He was an electrician, and as he would say, "I put lights in." My father dressed really nice. My father loved beer and he introduced us to papaya juice. I love papaya juice. He also loved driving nice clean cars. He loved Cadillacs. Before he died he was driving a white Lincoln Town car with burgundy leather seats. My father was about 6' 2" tall. He enjoyed going to the race track with his mother. He would do all the clothes shopping for us when we were kids. He would buy all name brand clothes.

My father died on June 26, 1996 at St. Louis University Hospital. His funeral was small. He really was a private man for the most part. He would sometimes have sunglasses on while in the hospital … I guess he didn't want anybody to see him.

My father gave his life to Christ while sick. I know
he is heaven and we will see each other again. Before
Christ, my daddy's voice was very loud and he knew
how to use curse words. My dad was shot multiple times
in the stomach when we were kids. I don't know what
happened, I just know he was shot. My father did leave
some unfinished business here.

Please keep important information updated.

For the most part, I had a good dad and I knew he loved
all his kids. He loved Marvin Gaye and Sugar Ray
Leonard and he compared himself with Muhammad Ali
because he had twins too. I miss my daddy and I wish I
had more time with him. He died when I was 24. Every
daughter needs their father.

My Strength Is Your Strength

22 | PRINCESS QUITE-A-LOT / MAMA

My mother is a two-time breast cancer survivor as well.
She survived breast cancer at the age of 36 and 56.

Mama's two breast cancers were 20 years apart in the
same breast. My mother is a very private person so she
rarely talks about her journey. My mother says, "I am not
giving cancer any credit." My mother was working at a
large corporation when she was diagnosed with breast
cancer the first time, however, her employer treated her
so badly because of the side effects of chemotherapy,
which included – hair loss, nausea, vomiting, severely
decreased appetite, extreme fatigue, anemia, and her nail
beds turned a bluish color.

Due to the mistreatment she received while working,
my mother decided to follow her passion which was
becoming a manicurist. My mother has been doing nails
for over 20 years now. She opened her first nail salon in
Ferguson, Missouri. She named it N2 Nails Salon. My
mother has had some of the same clients for over 20
years. She is now a mobile manicurist. I was one of my
mother's caregivers during her second bout with breast
cancer. My mother's faith has always being tested but

her faith is RIDICULOUS. Whatever my mother puts her mind to or whatever she believes can happen ... IT HAPPENS! I remember my mother purchasing a car in my childhood for only $40.00. She drove this station wagon until she was ready to purchase another vehicle. Her Faith. Her Belief. Wow!!

My mother decided to get tested for the gene mutation. She tested BRCA2 positive. I inherited breast cancer from my mother. After I was diagnosed with breast cancer the second time, my breast surgeon requested that my mother have this test done. She then had preventative surgery since the test results came back positive.

My mother is a very quiet woman and does not reveal her emotions easily. I don't know if that's strength or something else. On the other hand, I am a crybaby. I have never heard my mother curse either. My mother has always been in church, and in my childhood there were times where we actually slept at church all night praying with the congregation. My mother is not just a church goer. She believes in paying tithes and working in the church. She believes in the Holy Spirit and its guidance. My mother works as a greeter in the church.

I definitely don't want to make it look like my mother is all church. She also loves to dance and boy can she dance. My aunt once said, "When my sister was younger, people used to ask her and pay her to dance." She has her own style of dancing. She also loves interior design.

Her home looks like it should be in a magazine. You
walk into her bathroom and say, "Wow, how and why?"
She is definitely a woman of wisdom. I think a woman
that carried and raised twins is a special type of woman.
I have never heard my mother gossip or speak bad about
anyone. She dresses really nice and she will tell you …
"Just Accessorize."

My Strength Is Your Strength

MY STRENGTH IS ...

23 | GRANDPARENTS

We all need our grandparents. They teach us what
our parents forget to teach us. That's what I missed
out on. Fortunately, I did have my father's mother,
Pudding, until I was a teenager. She absolutely loved
her granddaughters. I never met my grandfather on
my father's side and I only met my grandfather on my
mother's side one time.

My Strength Is Your Strength

MY
STRENGTH IS ... _____

24 | EYELASHES – MY TWIN

Vanessa was born June 18, thirty minutes before me according to my mother. What took me so long to come out? Being a twin is so unique and special. You are first friends and then best friends. Of course, we also have our own set of friends – for balance. My twin and I talk on the phone every day, several times a day. All of our life we have been called each other's name. We are identical. Vanessa's name means butterfly.

I named the title of this chapter "Eyelashes" because my twin said to me after my second diagnosis, "I am going to have to get some **EYELASHES** and keep them on to prevent me from crying." This really hurt me. During this journey of breast cancer my sister said to me, "I asked God, why I couldn't have one of your cancer challenges?" I never would have thought or imagined someone saying that.

Because we are twins, Vanessa is BRCA2 positive too, but that is her story to tell.

During the time of my challenges my sister was going through a rocky marriage which resulted in a hurtful divorce and a loss of friends. There is nothing like having friends by your side while going through something. A phone call. An apology. A dinner date. A movie. Just something. I saw for myself, my sister literally went through this devastating time by herself. She had so many lonely days. As much as she wanted to be there for me, she couldn't. She lost friends and a husband during this time of her life. Unfortunately, she really didn't have a relationship with her in-laws. One of his family members came to their home to help him move, that was the extent of the relationship. One thing I personally learned from my sister's divorce is know the family you are marrying into. Nothing personal or bad to say, it's the truth. Never tell someone, "Just get over it" when they are going through a divorce. I remember my sister's words were, "Ain't nothing going back." My sister is strong. After her husband left, she invited some friends over to help her create a special room. A safe room. A place of healing and worship. She created a prayer room in her home. She painted it BRIGHT yellow ... because yellow is a "happy" color.

My twin and I were teenage parents at the same time. Our children were supposed to be born around the same time but I had my oldest son premature.

Vanessa is such a hard worker. She has worked two
jobs since I can remember. She has worked in the hotel
industry for 25 years, as of May 2017. Vanessa has just
about two of everything, including two cars and two jobs.
She is one blessed lady and sister.

My sister and I still dress alike by accident. My mother
always dressed us in red and blue when we were younger.
I always wore the blue. Most of the time we were dressed
alike. Growing up we always shared a room and had twin
size beds but we would always end up in the same bed.
That's what twins do. Me and my twin talk on the phone
several times a day. We both wear a size 8 shoe. I am a
little smaller than my twin but we have mainly been the
same size all of our adult life. We have a twin "super
power." We can give each other "the eye" and we both
know what the other is thinking. We don't argue much
but have had our moments. One thing is for sure, we have
each other's backs no matter what!

We both are left handed. My only aunt on my father's
side, Moné, made sure we were left-handed. I remember
Vanessa telling me when we were younger that I "write
messy." I have practiced and practiced writing neatly.
I think it's neat now. Practice makes almost perfect,
because nothing on earth is perfect.

If you know us then you know we have nicknames for
each other. I call my twin "Sau." My nickname is "Dee."

I have never called my twin by her first name. My mother
said when we were babies she would hear us talking to
each other in our own language and that's where "Dee"
and "Sau" came from. No one calls me Dee but my
twin. In school Sau was known as the 'good twin' and
I was known as the 'bad twin.' Sau was known as the
'smaller twin' and I was known as the 'bigger twin'. Sau
was known as the 'quiet twin' and I was known as the
'loud' twin. In middle school and high school we were
also known as the "fighting twins." We had our share of
fights in school. It seemed like we were either liked or
hated in school. To be light skinned, beautiful and long-
haired was not always popular and still not popular today.
"Pretty hurts," in my BeYonce voice. Fact though ... to
know us is to really love us. If you are not a friend of
ours you are missing some friends.

We were raised in a Christian home with only Christian
music. Unfortunately, we were thumb suckers too. My
mother said her ultrasound showed both of us sucking
our thumbs. I stopped sucking my thumb at the age of
21. The truth will set you free. I don't know when my
twin stopped sucking her thumb. There is a special bond
that twins have and I believe it begins at birth or while
in the womb. I absolutely love my younger sister, Diana
who is ten years younger than us, but since Sau and I
were teenage mothers together and life has happened, I
have more memories with my twin. We all have the same
mother and father.

Because my twin and I were teenage mothers, my mother got us our first apartment together after graduating from high school. My twin and I have been living independently since the age of 17. We learned very quickly that we could not live together any longer. I believe we lived together for less than six months. We were immature but even today I still don't think I could live with my twin. Well maybe.

We are alike but different. Being a twin is so unique. I feel my twin's pain and her strengths. Even when nobody is there for you, you have your twin. Thank God for twins.

With a recent report from the U.S. Centers for Disease Control and Prevention (CDC) disclosing that more twins are being born in the United States now than ever before (birth rates have soared more than 70 percent in the past 30 years), there's going to be a lot more pairs to go around.

Did you know?
- Identical twins do not have identical fingerprints.
- Massachusetts has the most twin births of any state in America.
- Mirror image identical twins have reverse asymmetric features.
- Twins interact with each other in the womb.
- Forty percent of twins invent their own language. (Dee and Sau did.)
- Women who eat a lot of dairy are prone to

conceiving twins.
- Mothers of twins may live longer.
- Tall women are more likely to have twins.
- The state with the lowest rate of twin births is New Mexico.
- Identical twins do not always have the same genetics.

My Strength Is Your Strength

25 | VALEDA

My pastor, Aeneas Williams, mentioned one Sunday in 2014 that everyone should know the meaning of their name.

The name, Valeda is a Latin baby name. In Latin the meaning of the name Valeda is brave. Quite ironic, I think I am pretty brave. The name Valeda is ranked in the 68,469th position of the most used names. That means that my name is rarely used. It is not a popular first name. People having the name Valeda appear to be originating from all over the world. There are 1,300 persons in the world that have my same name. The name Valeda has six characters which means that it is relatively medium-length compared to other names.

I, Valeda Keys, love wearing my hair in a bun. My hair has been long and thick all of my life. I have had it cut several times. I honestly love long hair and I am thankful to have hair. One of the main questions that is asked of me often is, "Did I lose my hair with cancer?" No, I didn't lose my hair but while in radiation therapy the left side of my hair felt thinner. My hair stylist at the time told me that while I was going through "my challenge" as

I prefer to call it, she wasn't going to put any chemicals in my hair. As a result, I haven't had any chemicals in my hair for about four years or more now.

I absolutely love salmon. I cook salmon weekly. Recipe is so easy ... just bake for 37 minutes at 370 degrees. Makes almost perfect salmon. Nothing is perfect but God, but my salmon recipe is close. I do not like exercising but I have to. I love ice cream and strawberry shakes. I also love potatoes. I love getting manicures and pedicures. What I don't like is when I go to the nail places and I can't understand what the manicurist is saying. I don't like acrylic nails but I will wear them for special occasions, just for the length. I do not like cold weather at all. I like high heels but nowadays I will take a nice tennis shoe over a high heel any day. Have fun in high heels while you can. Eventually you will trade them out for tennis shoes.

Some of the information in this chapter came from a Google search.

My Strength Is Your Strength

26 | GALLBLADDER SURGERY

Gallstones are also called cholelithiasis. It requires a medical diagnosis to confirm you have a gallstone. Pain areas are in the back or upper-right abdomen.

A pain started in January, 2011 on the right side of my stomach ... I couldn't eat hardly anything. The only thing I was able to eat was baked tilapia and spinach. I ended up losing a few pounds prior to this surgery because my side would hurt really bad if I ate something, especially if it was something spicy. I also had an episode of vomiting. I initially thought it was food poisoning or a stomach virus from all the holiday Christmas parties and holiday eating I had been doing. I was originally supposed to have my hysterectomy in the year of 2011 due to the BRCA2 gene mutation results. I ended up being referred to a great gastroenterologist whom is now retired. I was referred by my primary physician, Christian Wessling, M.D., who played a major part in my physician decision-making process for all of my medical concerns. Dr. Wessling has referred me to some of the best doctors around.

My neighbor, an older retired lawyer once told me, "I

have had so many surgeries and the key to them all is to have the best surgeon." I was told I had one large irritated gallstone which resulted in the removal of my entire gallbladder. My surgery was March, 2011. It was supposed to be a same-day surgery, I ended up staying overnight because I came out of anesthesia vomiting and the doctors wanted to keep me overnight. My blood was drawn twice but the tubes were mislabeled. By the way, I am a very hard patient to draw blood from. My veins roll and are very small/thin. If you use a butterfly needle, you can get my blood. I am always hoping for a good phlebotomist. I only let you stick me one time, so you have to do a good job the first time.

My Strength Is Your Strength

27 | TRAM DELAY SURGERY

This was surgery #5.

I was getting pretty familiar with surgeries, less anxiety. This surgery was done by my plastic surgeon. This is the surgery done two weeks before the actual TRAM surgery and is required for a successful transverse rectus abdominis myocutaneous (TRAM) flap breast reconstruction.

I asked Dr. Maclin, my plastic surgeon, "What are the most important things he would say about the TRAM delay procedure?" He said, "The TRAM delay is a procedure where you cut the blood vessels early to force the flap to develop bigger vessels. So it is an investment in getting more of the flap to survive and fewer complications. It's routine when I do TRAMS and significantly minimizes flap complications."

This surgery was not so bad. I was off work for a few days. I experienced cramps afterwards. I took Ibuprofen and just took it easy. Dr. Maclin always performs

surgeries on a Thursday, so I would take Friday off from work and if you have weekends off, these can be considered healing and resting days without pay. I only had so many paid time off (PTO) days so I planned my surgeries, as best as I could, around a weekend.

My Strength Is Your Strength

28 | THE TRAM SURGERY

This was the second to worst surgery out of all seven surgeries I had during this journey. This was surgery #6. My plastic surgeon told me it will take one year to heal from this surgery. It took exactly one year for me to be able to somewhat comfortably lay and sleep on my side. To this day I still can't really sleep on my stomach. I sleep on my left side.

This surgery was about 9 hours long. In fact this surgery was so long, my plastic surgeon told me he had to change shoes during the surgery. My hospital stay was about a week. Your stay could be longer or shorter depending on fever or infection, which may or may not occur. I had six drains. SIX! UGH … refer back to chapter 18, Them Damn Drains!

In order to be eligible for this surgery you must be under 200 pounds for safety reasons for both you and the surgeons. I was over 200 pounds so I had to lose weight. I did that! I lost the weight with exercise and diet. I would have 600 calories in the morning and 600 calories in the evening. I didn't eat chips for about a year and I

drank lots of water. Two days a week I would exercise for two hours. I was in the Livestrong exercise program recommended for cancer survivors and their caregivers.

With this surgery, you are cut from hip to hip and reconstruction starts to take place. Once the surgery is finally over, the only comfortable position is laying on your back and sleeping and resting in a recliner while recovering. Wearing a binder and girdle after this surgery really helps. You are sent home from the hospital with a binder on. The binder itself gets worn out after wearing it for some time. When you need a new one you have to pay for it out-of-pocket. I would wear my girdle every day. It made me feel so much better, after all, so many muscles were tangled with during this surgery. During the TRAM flap surgery, an incision is made along your bikini line and an oval section of skin, fat, blood vessels, and muscle is taken from the lower half of your belly, moved up to your chest, and formed into a your new breast shape. You'll likely have to take care of three incisions on your new breasts: your lower abdomen, around your belly button and more than likely you will have drains in your reconstructed breast and in your abdominal site. You can't lift anything heavy, no strenuous sports and no sexual activity for six weeks. You should also consume protein with this surgery, it helps with your healing. The protein powder can be purchased at Walmart. It isn't expensive. Cost is around $20. I would take the "physician recommended amount" which for me was two scoops every morning with juice, because I didn't think it tasted too good with water.

Surgery #6 was one of the worst, or should I say complicated, surgeries I have ever had. I pray to God that I don't have any surgeries like that ever again. I really didn't have a choice with this surgery due to the fact I had breast cancer before and the radiation destroyed my skin. I could have opted not to have reconstruction surgery, but I wasn't ready for that either since I couldn't imagine waking up to a flat chest every morning. Everyone thinks differently. The good thing about the TRAM surgery is that in ten years you will not have to return to get implants replaced because your breasts have been reconstructed by your own tissue.

A bonus is, it does appear that you have had a tummy tuck. I felt like I had a tummy tuck. I loved the results but I hated the recovery. I have a new navel too ... my surgeon made it smaller, well let's just say it has been recreated and re-sited. This surgery is not recommended if you smoke, plan on getting pregnant, have had multiple abdominal surgeries or you are a thin woman who doesn't have enough extra belly tissue. This surgery also involves much support. You will need to sleep and rest in a recliner until the drains are gone and you feel like you can sleep on your stomach. Unfortunately, I got an infection a week after this surgery, which required a hospital stay. I was sent home with IV antibiotics that I had to administer myself. Luckily, I am a nurse. Because of the nature of this surgery, I was once again required to sleep in a recliner.

My Strength Is Your Strength

MY STRENGTH IS ... _____

29 | THE INFECTION

Signs of Infection – Whether you're recovering from surgery or injury, it is important to keep an eye out for a possible wound infection. Even when you take all the necessary steps to prevent an infection, one can still develop. If you notice any of the following signs, don't ignore them! See your doctor for the infected wound, and don't wait. The sooner you see your doctor for an infection, the better.

1. **Feelings of Malaise/Tired:** Malaise is a common non-specific sign of localized systemic infection. It is a feeling of tiredness and a lack of energy. This is exactly how I felt when trying to take a shower with the assistance of my husband. Even with his assistance I felt extremely tired and weak. This was after my 6th surgery (TRAM surgery), a week after leaving the hospital. I knew something was wrong and I couldn't IGNORE it.

2. **Running a Fever:** If your temperature reaches 101 degrees or more; it may be an indication that you have an infection.

3. **Fluid Drainage:** It is normal to have some fluid

drainage from the incision area after surgery. Expect the fluid to be clear or slightly yellow. If the drainage fluid is cloudy, green or has a foul odor, this could be a sign that the wound is infected.

4. **Continual or Increased Pain:** Pain is common after surgery, but it should gradually go away as the body heals. If you continue to experience pain or suddenly have increased pain, it may be a sign of infection. Don't ignore constant pain. Connect with your physician.

5. **Redness and Swelling:** Some redness is normal at the wound site, but it should disappear over time. However, if your surgical incision or wound continues to be red, you could have an infection. Do not ignore redness and/or swelling but instead call your doctor.

6. **Hot Incision Site:** When an infection develops in a wound or incision the body sends infection-fighting blood cells to the location. This may make your wound or incision feel warm to the touch. Do not ignore this sign if the hotness continues.

My Strength Is Your Strength

30 | NIPPLE RECONSTRUCTION

Let me just be honest ... and nothing against my plastic
surgeon ... but this surgery was wasted time. I thought
I was going to have these perky nipples. I don't have
perky nipples! My new nipples ... they don't stick out. In
fact, you really can't tell I even had nipple reconstruction
surgery. The bright side is, I am glad I did have this
surgery because if I didn't have this surgery I wouldn't
be able to tell you about my experience. So despite the
"wasted time," I don't have any regrets. I definitely try to
live life with few regrets.

The surgery itself is not complicated at all, at least not
compared to everything else I had already been through.
I was off work, I think, for only two weeks. This was
surgery #7 within 2 years. July, 2013. Thankfully, it
was my last surgery. After this surgery you come home
with your breast area in bandages. Once the bandages
come off your nipples do look perky but over time they
begin to look smashed, so that's what I mean by wasted
time. Who wants smashed nipples after all you've
been through? And honestly, having my nipples perky
wasn't really for my satisfaction anyway, it was for my

husband's so I felt disappointed for him that this surgery was not a huge success.

Technology is always improving though so let's just hope there is a better way to keep the nipples perky one day in the near future.

My Strength Is Your Strength

31 | MY DOCTORS

Let me just say this, when it comes to your health, you must feel comfortable with your doctors. You must be able to ask questions and receive answers. After being diagnosed with breast cancer, two things came immediately to my mind: Death and Pain. If you are not satisfied with your doctors, do something different. Ask family and friends who they see or who they would recommend. Of course, Google search, "Best Plastic Surgeon In [Wherever You Live]." The main thing is that you're comfortable with your doctors. This recommendation is for you even if you are not diagnosed with breast cancer, or any cancer for that matter. It is just a good rule of thumb, for general health … you must be comfortable with your doctors. I can't stress it enough, if you are not comfortable with your doctors **MOVE ON**.

I can honestly say during my challenge with breast cancer, I was very satisfied with the my entire team of doctors. Here is a list of my doctors and I would recommend them to you.

Christian Wessling, MD – Family Practice
7979 Big Bend Blvd.
Webster Groves, MO 63119
(314) 961-6631

Our family visits annually. In order to have a mammogram, you must have a physician's order. You must see a physician at least annually. Dr. Wessling is quiet, tall, drinks green tea daily and is very resourceful. He is quiet only because he is thinking of a great master plan.

Gregory W. Uelk, DMD – Dentist
11705 Dorsett Rd.
Maryland Heights, MO 63043
(314) 739-4100

It is important to get your teeth cleaned every six months. Clean teeth equals clean breath.

Laura A. Baalmann, MD – FACOG – Obstetrician and Gynecologist (OB-GYN)
Balanced Care For Women
10806 Olive Blvd.
St. Louis, MO 63141
(314) 993-7009

Dr. Baalmann specializes in the woman's reproductive tract, pregnancy and childbirth. She also can refer you to a physician that specializes in hysterectomies if you have the BRCA2 gene mutation.

Diane Radford, MD – Breast Surgeon
Cleveland Clinic Main Campus
9500 Euclid Ave.
Cleveland OH 44195
(216) 444-3024

She has relocated and is no longer in St. Louis, MO
but if you are reading my book in Cleveland, OH I
highly recommend Dr. Radford. Dr. Radford performed
my lumpectomy and double mastectomy. She is very
thorough. She draws pictures of the size of your cancer
and explains everything to your understanding.

Dr. Nishan H. Chobanian, Jr., MD – Gynecology
Oncology & Obstetrics & Gynecology
St. John Providence
26850 Providence Parkway, Suite 402
Novi, MI 48374
(248) 849-8607

He has also relocated and is no longer in St. Louis,
MO but I can highly recommend him if you are in the
Novi, MI area. He is very thorough. He performed my
hysterectomy, which was my da Vinci Surgery (Robotic-
Assisted) due to the BRCA2 gene mutation.

Susan L. Luedke, MD – Medical Oncology
St. Louis Cancer & Breast Institute
6435 Chippewa St.
St. Louis, MO 63109
(314) 353-1870

Dr. Luedke is what I call an "old school physician." She
has great bedside manners. She tells it like it is in a very
professional manner. You can tell she really enjoys her
work and is very passionate about what she does. For me
she prescribed and monitored the medication Tamoxifen
which I took for one year and 5 five days. Dr. Luedke is
a wonderful doctor however I've heard she is about to
retire. Job Well Done, Dr. Luedke!!!!

Dr. Melvin M. Maclin, II, MD – Board Certified Plastic
Surgeon
Parkcrest Plastic Surgery
845 N. New Ballas Ct., Suite 300
St. Louis, MO 63141
(314) 485-4965

Dr. Maclin has been recognized as one of St. Louis'
prestigious "Top Doctors" in Plastic and Reconstructive
Surgery since 2008. Dr. Maclin is comical, he has great
bedside manners and of course, he's handsome and
married. Dr. Maclin has been a keynote speaker for
Valeda's Hope Pink and Pearls Luncheon.

Kathy L. Baglan, MD – Radiation Oncology
West County Radiological Group
15945 Clayton Road, Suite 100
Ballwin, MO 63011
(314) 251-6844

Dr. Baglan is a twin also… how ironic!!! Her twin is a
radiation oncologist too.

Dr. Lannis Hall, MD, MPH – Radiation Oncology
Siteman Cancer Center at Barnes-Jewish St. Peters
Hospital
150 Entrance Way
Saint Peters, MO 63376
(636) 916- 9920.

Dr. Hall is consistently recognized on "The Best Doctors
in America" list. She has been a keynote speaker for
Valeda's Hope Pink & Pearls Luncheon for multiple
years.

Jovita Oruwari, MD – General Surgery, Breast Surgery
St. Louis Cancer & Breast Institute
15945 Clayton Rd., Suite #120
Chesterfield, MO 63005
(636) 256-5000

Dr. Oruwari has also been a keynote speaker for Valeda's
Hope Pink & Pearls Luncheon.

Julie A. Margenthaler, MD – Breast Surgeon
Center for Advanced Medicine Breast Health Center
4921 Parkview Place
St. Louis, MO 63110
(314) 362- 7534

Dr. Margenthaler's area of clinical interest is in
breast cancer in young women less than 40 years
old. Dr. Margenthaler can also perform surgeries for
fibroadenoma. I hope my list of doctors helps you, if you
are looking for a new physician.

Things to consider when choosing a new doctor:
- When making appointments, please make sure
  your insurance is accepted by that physician.
- Ask if there are any co-payments you will be
  responsible for prior to making your appointment.
  Ask for assistance with payments if you need
  assistance.
- Just because you may be diagnosed with breast
  cancer doesn't mean you should NEGLECT
  the rest of your body. Make and keep all your
  appointments. Be consistent with your health!
- If you are instructed by a doctor not to drive to
  an appointment, procedure, or surgery DON'T
  DRIVE.
- I would recommend a physician that's close to
  your home or job. You may have to catch a cab or
  have limited time to make it to your appointment
  so make it less stressful for yourself.

- If you are in a relationship, your mate should also see a physician regularly. If your mate doesn't see a physician regularly ... EVALUATE THE RELATIONSHIP. If your mate doesn't care about his or her health, why should you?
- If your spouse is not supportive, evaluate the relationship. You don't need someone only when you can put your pajamas on independently, you need them when you CAN'T put them on. "Thank you hubby for taking care of me when I couldn't take care of myself."

My Strength Is Your Strength

MY
STRENGTH IS ... _____

32 | QUESTIONS TO ASK DOCTORS

1. How long is my surgery?
2. How long is the hospital stay?
3. Can you pre-order my pain medications at my pharmacy? Helpful Hint: When you are in pain you don't feel like WAITING to pick up your medication, you want it as soon as you arrive at the pharmacy.
4. What is your after-hours contact information?
5. Will you be on vacation after my surgery?
6. What is your email address?
7. What is your assistant's email address?
8. How will I look after surgery? What should I expect post-op? Ask to see pictures.
9. When is the best time to call you if I have any questions?
10. How long have you've been in practice?
11. How long is recovery?
12. How do I sleep?
13. Will I need a recliner?
14. What are some of the side effects to prescribed medications?
15. What is the diagnosis again? DO YOUR RESEARCH!

16. What is the size of my cancer?
17. What stage is my cancer? What do the stages mean?
18. What is my prognosis?

My Strength Is Your Strength

33 | BREAST CANCER STAGES

Once you find out you have breast cancer, your healthcare team will tell you what stage you're in. For both of my cancers, I was in stage 0. Thank God! After my surgeries and getting through my "breast cancer challenge," I started Valeda's Hope, a 501(c)(3) Not-For Profit (NFP) organization. I have received many calls at Valeda's Hope from women who don't really know what their stage means and call just to learn more.

The stage is very important for two reasons:

1. It helps define the best way to contain the cancer.
2. It helps define the best way to eliminate the cancer.

The stage is based on the size of the tumor in the breast and the number of lymph nodes found under your arm, known as the axillary area or signs, indicating whether the breast cancer has spread to other organs within the body.

Metastasize: the breast cancer has spread to other sites in the body

Stages 0 & 1 – This represents the earliest detection of breast cancer development. At stages 0 & 1, the cancer cells are confined to a very limited area. (This is the stage you want if this is part of your challenge). The treatment options you will have are broader and wider.

Stage 2 – You are still in the early stages, but there is evidence that the cancer has begun to grow or spread. It is still contained to the breast area and it's treatable.

Stage 3 – It is considered advanced cancer with evidence of cancer invading surrounding tissues near the breast (lymph nodes).

Stage 4 – This indicates that cancer has spread beyond the breast to other areas of the body (brain, bones, lungs, liver).

At the end of the day, we must be accountable for our bodies. We must make and keep our mammogram appointments, just as we would our teeth cleaning and well-woman exam. We must not ignore anything that looks or feels abnormal. Of course, you want to always have medical insurance ... it's just like having life insurance and car insurance.

REMEMBER, EARLY DETECTION IS YOUR BEST PROTECTION.

My Strength Is Your Strength

34 | ITEMS NEEDED BEFORE & AFTER SURGERY

1. Bible
2. Your cell phone & charger – Obviously, you can't have your phone during surgery, however give it to someone that can answer questions appropriately on your behalf. People do care for you so let them help.
3. Button-down gown – This is a must if you are having a double mastectomy.
4. FMLA – Family Medical Leave Absence
5. Mints – Fresh breath means fresh conversations.
6. Magazines – Never get bored while healing.
7. Your doctor's after hours contact information.
8. Slippers – Take your own slippers to the hospital.
9. Bedside commode – Sometimes you can't get to your bathroom quick enough once you get home.
10. Remote control for TV
11. A meal plan —For three weeks at least.
12. A journal – Recording your feelings and emotions as you journey through your challenge is helpful, healing and therapeutic.
13. Back scratcher – Whoever invented back scratchers, "Thank you!"

14. Plenty of fiber (Cantaloupe!) – When you are not moving around as much and are taking certain medications you become constipated.
15. Prune juice – See #14.
16. Protein powder – Helps promote healing.
17. Floss
18. Transportation – You will need a designated driver(s). Consider your options: family member, friend, cab services, call-a-ride, Uber, etc.
19. Small pillows – For elevation and all-around comfort
20. Blanket – Bring your favorite!
21. Disposable underwear – Ask for these prior to surgery.
22. Pantyliners
23. Psychologist/counselor – I recommend finding someone that has been through what you've been through. Spend time with them prior to your surgery so you know they will be a good source of support for you after your surgery.
24. Cancer insurance
25. Before & after photos – These are important. They will help you mourn what you've lost and then help you move on and heal.
26. Benadryl
27. Antibacterial soap
28. Hand sanitizer – Take some to your hospital room for yourself and your visitors.
29. Comb & brush – "Looking pretty helps you feel pretty."

30. Hand towels
31. Toothbrush, toothpaste & mouthwash
32. Small luggage on wheels for hospital visit
33. Change of clothes
34. Reliable babysitter for small children
35. Contact your child's school officials, teachers, tutors, coaches, girl scout leaders, dance instructors, etc. Let them know what is going on so they can help support your child during this stressful time. Remember, cancer affects the whole family and kids need support too.
36. Contact your church family: pastor, pastor's wife, health ministries
37. Complete your grocery shopping before your surgery. Think about what "treats" you might like while you are recovering.
38. Stock up on prepared meals and microwave dinners
39. Bottled water – As always, drink lots and lots of water.

My Strength Is Your Strength

MY STRENGTH IS ... _____

35 | HEALING SCRIPTURES

Isaiah 53:5
But he was wounded for our transgressions, he was bruised for our iniquities: the chastisement of our peace was upon him; and with his stripes we are healed. (This is my Mama's favorite scripture.)

Psalm 118:17
I shall not die, but live, and declare the works of the Lord. (This is my daily affirmation.)

Isaiah 41:10
So do not fear, for I am with you, do not be dismayed, for I am your God. I will strengthen you and help you.

James 5:14
Is anyone among you sick? Let them call the elders of the church to pray over them and anoint them with oil in the name of the Lord.

Matthew 11:28
Come to me all you who are weary and burdened, and I will give you rest.

Phillipians 4:19
And my God will meet all your needs according to the riches of his glory in Christ Jesus.

Proverbs 4:20-22
My son, pay attention to what I say, turn your ear to my words. Do not let them out of your sight, keep them within your heart. For they are life to those who find them and health to one's whole body.

Exodus 23:25
Worship the Lord your God, and his blessing will be on your food and water, I will take away sickness from among you.

Psalms 30:2
Lord my God, I called to you for help, and you healed me.

Psalms 147:3
He heals the brokenhearted and binds up their wounds.

Jeremiah 17:14
Heal me Lord, and I will be healed, save me and I will be saved, for you are the one I praise.

Matthew 9:35
Jesus went through all the towns and villages, teaching in their synagogues, proclaiming the good news of the kingdom and healing every disease and sickness.

Mark 5:34

He said to her daughter your faith has healed you, go in peace and be freed from your suffering.

James 5:16

Therefore confess your sins to each other and pray for each other so that you may be healed. The prayer of a righteous person is powerful and effective.

My Strength Is Your Strength

MY STRENGTH IS ... _____

36 | RESOURCES

Susan G. Komen
www.info-komen.org

Gateway To Hope
www.gthstl.org

St. Louis Men's Group Against Cancer
www.stlmgac.com

Valeda's Hope
www.valedashope.org

Dr. Susan Love Research Foundation –
www.drsusanloveresearch.org

American Cancer Society
www.cancer.org

The Food Outreach
www.foodoutreach.org

The Pink Daisy Project (for women under the age of 45)
www.pinkdaisyproject.com

The Cancer Care Foundation
www.cancercare.org

Schnuck's Pharmacy/ Ladue Pharmacy
www.laduepharmacy.com

Medical West Breast Prosthesis Center
www.medicalwest.com

Home Affordable Modification Program (HAMP)
www.hmpadmin.com

American Cancer Society Hope Lodge
www.cancer.org

The Gracie Foundation
www.thegraciefoundation.org

Cleaning For A Reason
www.cleaningforareason.org

National Cancer Comprehensive Network
www.nccn.org

The Comprehensive Patient Navigation Guide
9th Edition Breast Cancer Treatment Handbook
by Judy C. Kneece, RN, OCN

Program for Elimination of Cancer Disparities (PECad)
publichealthsciences.wustl.edu/community-focus/program-for-elimination-of-cancer-disparities

My Strength Is Your Strength

37 | WACOAL BRAS – MY NEW BEST [GIRLS'] FRIEND

In July 2013, after losing "my girls" due to my second battle with breast cancer, and my seventh surgery I realized I wanted new bras to make me feel comfortable and pretty, and I needed new bras to properly cup and support my new breasts. I was volunteering for the Wacoal Fit for the Cure at Macy's – Susan G. Komen St. Louis in the intimate apparel department when I met my "new best [*girls'*] friend."

As a gift for volunteering, a Wacoal Fit Specialist measured my new breasts and professionally fit me for a new bra. I was delighted when I received a new Wacoal Awareness Bra in the mail just a short time later. It was my first Wacoal bra and I immediately fell in love with the comfort, coverage, and beautiful design. And perhaps the most important thing, in addition to being a great bra, is that the Wacoal brand brings education and awareness to breast cancer in a unique, winning way. The Wacoal Awareness Bra is the only bra I wear and I highly recommend it. It is my way of looking good, feeling pretty and giving back at the same time through Wacoal's partnership with the Susan G. Komen organization. #Wacoal

My Strength Is Your Strength

MY STRENGTH IS ... _____

38 | BLOOD TYPE A

It is very important to know your blood type. My blood type is A+. This blood type thrives on a vegetarian diet with some wild caught fish. We have naturally high levels of the stress hormone cortisol. Cortisol is a hormone involved in the regulation of metabolism in the cells and helps us regulate stress within the body. Stress reduction is an essential part of the Type A lifestyle. We have to incorporate calming exercises such as yoga or tai chi into our lives. Type A's are predisposed to cardiovascular disease and other stress-related conditions. I truly believe stress played a huge part in my second diagnosis of breast cancer. As a result, I try to stay away from stressful situations, environments and people.

Our diet is supposed to be largely vegetarian: vegetables, tofu, seafood, grains, legumes, fruit and turkey. We must stay away from things like meat, dairy, kidney beans, lima beans, wheat, and corn. We benefit from olive oil, soy, seafood, vegetables, and pineapple. This plays a huge part in weight loss. I highly recommend for you to know your blood type.

Book Recommendations:
Eat Right 4 Your Type by Dr. Peter J. D'Adamo

There Are 4 Blood Types:
O Type, A Type, B Type, AB Type

Don't know your blood type? You should. Here's why:
- Your blood type determines the food you should eat and your susceptibility to illness.
- It is a factor in your energy levels and the efficiency in which you burn calories.
- Blood type plays a role in your stress response and allows you to create an exercise plan that's most effective for you.

My Strength Is Your Strength

39 | WINNING WAYS TO COPE WITH CANCER

I did all of these things, to keep me NORMAL:
- Get a massage (get your doctor's approval though) – I didn't get doctor's approval, oops!
- Meditate through Insight Timer App.
- Meditate on God's Word (Psalms 118:17).
- Talk with someone that's going through the same thing.
- Visit the sick (if you're not sick).
- Volunteer for a Not-For-Profit Organization such as ours: (Valeda's Hope) www.valedashope.org
- Listen to your favorite uplifting song (Whitney Houston – I Didn't Know My Own Strength).
- Pray without stopping (1 Thessalonians 5:16-18).
- Go to a comedy show. Laughter is good for the soul!
- Keep a journal.
- Attend weekly church services.
- Subscribe to your favorite magazine – *Essence, Redbook, Elle, Heart & Soul, Good Housekeeping, Oprah Magazine, Gazelle Magazine and Ebony Magazine.*
- Spend time with family and friends.

- Schedule times to cry, but remember, don't put too much pity in the party.
- Tell your story – It's healing.
- Speak positive affirmations daily over your life, body and future.
- Watch your words that come out of your mouth. Speak only positive words. If you don't have anything good to say, say NOTHING.
- Take a mini vacation if your body allows it.
- Take a long walk if you can in your neighborhood or local park.
- Register for a yoga class.
- Acupuncture.
- Don't be afraid to ask for help.
- Go to the movies.
- Accept help.
- Get a manicure and pedicure.
- Be nice.
- If you are not having chemotherapy treatments, get your hair done.
- Buy a new lipstick/lip gloss.
- Shop wisely.
- Live life one SECOND at a time, not DAY at a time. (I've learned with cancer your entire life can change in a matter of seconds.)
- Don't compare your cancer to someone else's cancer. Every cancer is different.

My Strength Is Your Strength

40 | FRIENDS

My mother always said, "If you have at least one friend, you are in good shape." I don't have many friends. I believe a lot of people like me as a person and I know a lot of people but it's a small circle that I would call "true friends." To say you are a friend is definitely an earned word. You truly find out who your friends are when cancer happens, divorce happens, you get married, you have a baby, even when death happens. Social media makes making new friends hard. You see so many 20 or 30 year friendships and then there is a post along with the friendship that says, "NO NEW FRIENDS ALLOWED." How cruel is that? My motto is, "Old friends become family and new friends become close friends. Close friends are a blessing to your future." I can honestly say I appreciate my old friends and I am very grateful for my new friends that God has blessed me with. As you grow into self, new people come into your life. You attract who you've become. I repeat, "You attract who you've become." Ask yourself, "Who are you becoming"?

Growing up, there have always been cliques. The long hair, light-skinned, pretty girls tend to hang around each other. At least that was my perception. As you become more mature, long hair, being beautiful on the outside or

being light- skinned does not matter. LOYALTY matters.

A man who has friends must show himself to be friendly, but there is a friend who sticks closer than a brother. Proverbs 18:24 New King James Version (NKJV)

How do you become a friend to someone? Just be friendly and let God do the rest. The people that belong in your life will be in your life. Surround yourself with people that you feel love you and those you love. Be loyal. Be positive. Stick around when bad events happen in your friends' lives. Don't talk about your friends in a negative way. Discuss disagreements. Apologize and mean it. Avoid gossip. Just giggle. Go the extra mile for your friends. Send them a simple text or a handwritten note ... "I'm just thinking about you, I hope all is well."

Life happens and everyone is busy but you need friends. Keep your word. Your word is your bond. If you say something and don't follow through, then we can't be friends or you will be in "that row." That row is putting people where they belong in your life so your feelings won't be hurt. Some people belong in the front row and some people belong in the back row. Sad but true, some people don't have a row. Your audience matters. Life and friends are like a theater. We all have feelings. Don't hurt mine and I won't hurt yours. Sometimes closing chapters with people is okay too, it may be necessary, but make sure everything is done in decent order. Don't end friendships on social media or write about them in

your book because even though you may be helping
people you are also hurting people. A loved one literally
went into a deep depression after she learned a friend
had written about her in her book. To this day, there is
no reconciliation or apologies, which is very sad. Life is
short so make it a great one with great friends and family.

Strength Is Your Strength

MY STRENGTH IS ... _____

41 | TATTOOS

**Areola: a small circular area, in particular the ring of
pigmented skin surrounding a nipple**

I never have had a desire to have a tattoo until my
second diagnosis of breast cancer, having both breasts
removed and going through reconstruction. I always
thought to myself, "Why would I want to do something
that actually causes pain." In addition, I was taught that
as a Christian you are not supposed to mark on your
body. The bible mentions tattoos just once, in Leviticus
19:28, which says: "You must not put tattoo markings
upon yourselves." God gave this command to the nation
of Israel, thus setting them apart from the neighboring
peoples who marked their skin with the names or
symbols of their gods. (Deuteronomy 14:2). Watching
my twin Sau and cousin when we were in our 20s get
tattoos with tears streaming down their faces it just didn't
make any sense to me. I have always wanted to be on
the giving side of life which is what I think led me to
being a nurse. I have never wanted to be on the receiving
side of things. I pray to God I never have to receive

another surgery in my life. Seven surgeries is enough and complete in God's word.

Despite my childhood thoughts and beliefs, I decided to get new areolas by tattooing them on. Three years after my seventh surgery in July, 2013 was my nipple reconstruction. I couldn't believe that much time had passed by. My husband always said I looked fine the way things were, but I was tired of looking at the scarring every day. I felt like a woman, I just didn't completely look like a woman to me. The best thing about getting my tattoos was I couldn't feel anything!! Well, I should say ... "it's good and bad" because after reconstruction all your original breast sensations are gone. However, that works out well if you decide you want a tattoo on your breasts because it doesn't hurt!! Well ... except for when she did my wording, which is the title of my book, "My Strength is Your Strength." This was the painful part that reminded me why I never considered a tattoo. Just a reminder, a point to ponder, when your breasts are removed you also lose your areola, so basically your new breasts are all one color. Unless, you are a candidate for nipple sparing mastectomy, where the nipple and areola are left in place.

If you decide to get breast tattoos, to celebrate your "new self," consider making a party out of it. That's what I did!! Take your mama, your sister, your aunt, your niece. Mix in a few special friends. Take goodie bags for party favors and then lean on your special people for support,

comfort and nurturing while you get your tattoo. That's
what I did!!

After the "party" I threw for myself at the tattoo parlor,
I was excited to come home to show my husband my
new breasts. His initial response was, "but the areola …
[pause] … for some reason I thought you were going to
have more than that." And I thought to myself, "Dear
God, what else can be done to these breasts?" Of course,
I instantly started thinking about his response. After all I
was doing this for me, for him, for us. I thought long and
hard. I prayed. I cried. I laughed. And then … I came up
with my idea … a sunflower! A sunflower means life. A
sunflower was perfect for me!!! If I turned my areola into
a sunflower that would be bigger!

Now, the tattoo artist who did my areola, was
recommended to me by my plastic surgeon, and I didn't
really like her bedside manners. She didn't say much to
me. She didn't seem to care that this was a BIG deal to
me. She was not kind or caring and she didn't come off
as a nice woman. I was glad I had my BFF's with me.
I was glad I had decided to throw myself my "Breast
Tattoo Party." In the end, the cost was $250.00. It took 2
hours. And I learned, it's important to meet your tattoo
artist first and be sure you are going to like them.

My sunflowers were done by a male. I figured a man
knows how he would want his woman to look. [This was
approved by my husband of course.] My sunflowers took
three hours and the cost was $200.00. The guy was really
nice, and it was in a comfortable private setting. I like my

131

results and I have no regrets. I decided, "if it makes you feel better to get a tattoo after all you've been through ... GET THE TATTOO!!"

For all have sinned and fall short of the glory of God. Romans 3:23 (New International Version)

Tattoo Aftercare

- Remove bandage when you get home and wash your tattoo for the first time.
- Wash tattoo with a gentle liquid antibacterial soap for about 1 minute.
- Rinse off your tattoo with clean water.
- Pat dry with a paper towel. Never scrub.
- You will typically wash your tattoo 2-3 times a day.
- Apply a small amount of mild, fragrance-free lotion, such as Lubriderm. Less is more. Do not over lotion your tattoo.
- Do not pick or scratch your new tattoo.
- It will take roughly 3 to 4 weeks for your new tattoo to heal. Always keep it clean and moisturized.
- Showering is fine, but do not swim or get into a hot tub or bath with your healing tattoo.

My recommendation for your tattoo is:
9506a Lackland Road
Overland, MO 63114
(314) 736-1801 (Ask for Rick)

My Strength Is Your Strength

42 | MY CAREER

I have been a licensed practical nurse (LPN) since 1999.
I graduated from LPN school on February 14, 1997. I
was almost seven months pregnant with my second child
when I graduated from LPN school. Being an LPN has
been challenging. I can say it's been rewarding when
it comes to my own health. I also get paid more than
minimum wage. It does pay the bills. It is easy to find a
job. There seems to always be a job available in places
I wouldn't particularly like to work such as nursing
homes, where it seems they are always short-staffed and
overworked. My goal was to always have a 9 to 5 job
while in the nursing field and God has graciously granted
me that so while my children were in school, I was at work.

When I was diagnosed with breast cancer for the first
time, I was working two jobs. One was at a nursing home
on the weekends and some evenings. The nursing home
was right around the corner from my first job. I remember
telling God when I first became a nurse, "All I want to do
is make $20.00 an hour." How crazy!!!! I have made $20
an hour and I have made more than $20 an hour. What I
have learned is to give yourself a raise by becoming your

own boss. Raises are nothing coming from an employer. That has been my experience. I personally haven't had a raise on a job for more than five years. I GIVE more than I RECEIVE.

In everything I did, I showed you that by this kind of hard work we must help the weak, remembering the words the Lord Jesus himself said: "It is more blessed to give than to receive." Acts 20:35 (New International Version)

My years as a nurse have gone by so fast. I have learned a lot about myself, and people, and healthcare. Nursing is a field in which the majority of the workforce is women. It can be messy. I can honestly say that I have had a few disagreements in this field however. For the majority of people that I've worked with, I know my reputation is that I am a hard worker. I did return to school to become a registered nurse ... but ... then ... shingles happened.

I was in such a hurry for my cancer challenge to be over so I could move forward with my future but that didn't happen. Once I realized that my job for five years was very stressful ... I resigned – May, 2013. This was after my 6th surgery. I was working with troubled youth and some had mental issues. There were 600 students where I worked, ages 16-24 and only four nurses. The job itself was a very high-demand job but I didn't realize it until my second diagnosis. Every day was fast paced and there was always an emergency going on: fights, asthma attacks etc.

In June, 2013, I was hired at an infertility clinic. It is
a clinic for women that can't have children but want to
have children through In Vitro Fertilization (IVF). My
employer told me that she had more than 300 applicants
and God told her to hire me. I thought it was a God-
sent job because I would be working with women that
couldn't bear children and here I am BRCA2 positive and
have had a hysterectomy. I'm thinking to myself, this is
the perfect job. I felt I had something to offer the women
with my very own experiences. It was in Creve Coeur
which was a great location. It was right down the street
from my plastic surgeon's office, and I was still under his
care so this was ideal. In all of my jobs, I always wanted
my own private office and at the infertility clinic I had
one! It was beautiful! I even had a decent view from my
window.

For some reason though, in my spirit, it just didn't feel
like I would be there long. It didn't feel like home. As
much as I wanted this job to be my last stop, it wasn't.
My supervisor even told me to decorate my office and
I was thinking to myself, "I will decorate my office
when my probation period is up." As the days went by,
I noticed I was the only African American working in
my area. There was another African American woman
working in the medical records department, but I
was the only one in my area. A lot of pharmaceutical
representatives would come in and they would greet
me as if I was the supervisor. I think it was because
of the way I was dressed in uniform. I looked very

professional. The infertility clinic is a place where most of the patients were pretty wealthy, so I couldn't figure out why most all of the workers wouldn't come to work looking professional in my opinion. My co-workers just didn't dress to par, which was very surprising to me. My supervisor told me to dress casual in uniform and I did, but in a slightly more professional way. The job itself felt like the perfect job but something just didn't feel right to me. Long story short, I heard my supervisor in her office on the phone telling someone, "I will get rid of her tomorrow or the next day." I thought to myself. I am the newest employee here so she could only be talking about me. I went home and told my husband about what I had heard and he said, "Just go to work tomorrow and see what happens." Well, I went into work the next day and brought in McDonald's for everybody. Everyone refused.

I felt funny in my spirit, but I continued to work. I remember my supervisor leaving saying she would be back by noon. Well, by noon she was back and she told me to come to her office and sit down. I told her I was okay standing (remembering what I heard her say in her office the day before). She said two things to me, "I wasn't the perfect fit for the job and I didn't do anything wrong." She then asked me, "Did I have anything to say or any questions? I said to her, "You said God told you to hire me, right?" She said, "Yes, God did speak with me about you." She then handed me my last check and gave me some papers to sign which stated no reason for termination. I left and immediately called my husband.

He told me to go file for unemployment which I did
receive. I was fired on August 1, 2013. I was making $24
per hour which was the most I had ever made as a nurse
without holiday pay or overtime.

September 2014, I was hired at a women's health clinic.
I absolutely love working at clinics. As a nurse you
must find out what you love about being a nurse and
you must be comfortable with what you are doing. After
all, you spend most of your day at your job. My nurse
manager told me she hired me for my experience as a
breast cancer survivor and they are creating a position
for their mammogram program. Now, I really thought
this was the perfect job. What better way for me to give
back to the community AND get paid for it. I did have
my own office, but I didn't have a window and it was in
a bad neighborhood. Definitely a neighborhood I would
prefer to not work in or commute to daily. But nothing is
perfect. You have to take the good with the bad. I really
felt satisfied with the position.

By December, 2014, my supervisor job was no longer
available. By April 2015, my new position was no longer
available but I still had a job within the company working
with homeless men. This put me in a very depressed
state and I started to have panic attacks. I even had to go
see my primary care physician. He put me on another
anti-hypertensive medication because my blood pressure
was high. He put me on Atenolol, which I no longer
take. The Atenolol gave me daily joint pain. I had to

drive further into downtown St. Louis, in addition to me not liking what I was doing at all which was driving to different homeless shelters, and meeting the needs of the homeless. A lot of these homeless people had just gotten out of jail. I decided that working with the homeless is not for me. I truly feel sorry for the position they are in, but it's just not for me.

I enjoy meeting the needs of women. I was determined to work there until my son graduated from high school which was a couple of weeks away. May, 2015 ... two weeks before my youngest son Anthony graduated from high school my new position working with the homeless became no longer available.

In conclusion, I've quit a job, I've been fired from a job, and I've been laid off a job, all since my cancer challenge started. My advice is to strive to be your own boss, doing what you are passionate about while getting paid. That is my "hope" and "prayer" for myself and anyone that desires to do what they are passionate about.

My next challenge is to get my degree and become a registered nurse with an emphasis in oncology.

My Strength Is Your Strength

43 | FIBROADENOMA

I honestly didn't know anything about fibroadenoma until
my niece was diagnosed in 2016. She is the daughter
of my younger sister. She was 13 years of age with a
lump in her right breast the size of a golf ball. My niece
didn't ignore this. She immediately told her mother and
grandmother. My mother called me with the news and
we both had the same thought … "The devil is trying to
attack the youngest of us all." Her original surgery was
scheduled at Barnes-Jewish Hospital West however, there
was miscommunication regarding her age so her surgery
had to be rescheduled. She was 14 years old when she
had surgery which was performed at St. Louis Children's
Hospital in St. Louis, Missouri. Her surgery was outpatient surgery so she came home the same day with
bandages that she couldn't remove for two to three days.
She has a small scar which reminds her of her strength.
She was surrounded by family and friends before and
after her surgery who wanted to offer their support and
continual love. I was thinking to myself, "My niece is
so brave." She wasn't crying and never appeared to be
afraid however, after her surgery, she said she did cry
because her body felt like it had been through something.
My niece was wheeled to my sister's car in a wheelchair

after surgery. She spoke highly of Dr. Julie Margenthaler, saying, "Dr. Margenthaler knew exactly what it was and explained everything to me." Fortunately, my niece hasn't had any problems since surgery. The lump was noncancerous. Praise God! I asked her what message would she give other girls around her age. She said, "Be sure to do your monthly self breast exams and if you feel anything that's not normal tell someone immediately." I am so proud my niece didn't ignore this lump and she told us. This is another reason why my book wasn't completed sooner. I needed to write about fibroadenomas. God knows the beginning and the end. My niece was awarded the "My Strength is your Strength" award at Valeda's Hope 5th Annual Pink & Pearls Luncheon in October, 2016. She is the youngest of all the women and girls we've honored. She is a sophomore in high school and she desires to be an engineer.

So, what exactly is fibroadenoma? Fibroadenomas are solid, benign (non-cancerous) breast lumps that occur most often in women between the ages of 15 and 35.

A fibroadenoma might feel firm, smooth, rubbery or hard and has a well-defined shaped. Usually painless, it might feel like a marble in your breast, moving easily under your skin when examined. Fibroadenomas vary in size, and they can enlarge or shrink on their own.

Fibroadenomas are among the most common non-cancerous breast lumps in young women. Treatment might include monitoring to detect changes in size or feel, a biopsy to evaluate the lump, or surgery to remove it.

The cause of fibroadenomas is unknown, but they might be related to reproductive hormones. Fibroadenomas occur more often during your reproductive years, they can become bigger during pregnancy or with the use of hormone therapy, and might shrink after menopause, when hormone levels decrease. (The Mayo Clinic)

My Strength Is Your Strength

MY STRENGTH IS ... _____

44 | SEVEN

I have had a total of seven surgeries in the past seven years. I definitely didn't want to endure this as it related to the number seven. The number seven is the number that reflects my life. I believe most people have a favorite number, or a number that seems to stick out to their life. For me ... in addition to my seven surgeries, there is a seven-year age difference between my husband and I, my children were born seven years apart, and one of my telephone numbers has more than two sevens in it.

Seven is the number of completeness and perfection (both physically and spiritually). Much of its meaning is from being tied directly to God's creation of all things. There are seven days in a week and God's Sabbath is on the seventh day. The number seven is used 735 times in the Bible. (54 times in the book of Revelation alone), the number seven is the foundation of God's word. If we include with this count how many times 'sevenfold' (6) and 'seventh' (119) is used, the total jumps to 860 references. The number seven is one of the most significant numbers of the Bible because it is the number of spiritual perfection. The number seven is spiritual but

not religious. It is the number which is stamped on every work of God. Seven occurs 287 times in the scriptures 287 = 7 x 41.

The number seven is the seeker, the thinker, the searcher of Truth (notice the capital "T"). The seven doesn't take anything at face value — it is always trying to understand the underlying, hidden truths. The seven knows that nothing is exactly as it seems and that reality is often hidden behind illusions.

There are seven colors in the rainbow. Rainbows appear in seven colors because water droplets break white sunlight into the seven colors of the spectrum (red, orange, yellow, green, blue, indigo, violet). Now, I see why I don't have a favorite color. Did you know, you can only see a rainbow if the sun is behind you and the rain in front of you. There are seven Jewish feast days in the year, seven branches on the Menorah, seven Christian virtues, seven Hindu marriage vows, and seven chakra energy centers.

The number seven is often called "Lucky 7" and associated with Las Vegas slot machine winnings because seven is a sign that you are literally winning at life. Seven means, "You're on the right path, keep going forward in the direction you're heading."

In Angel Numbers, you may see 777 frequently, because the more 7's you see, the more encouragement you are receiving. The angels are cheering you on by showering you with the 7's, and they're supporting you all the way.

In many cultures around the world, seven is considered a lucky number. Whether the number seven is really lucky or not is a matter of opinion. Some people believe it is, but this may simply stem from the positive things often associated with the number.

Jesus performed seven miracles on God's Holy Sabbath Day (which ran from Friday sunset to Saturday sunset), affirming its continued sacredness to God and necessity in the life of the believer.

1. Jesus healed the withered hand of man attending synagogue services. (Matthew 12:9)
2. At a Capernaum synagogue He casts out an unclean spirit that possessed a man. (Mark 1:21)
3. Right after the above miracle Jesus heals Peter's wife's mother of a fever (Mark 1:29)
4. A woman attending synagogue, who was made sick by a demon for eighteen years, is released from her bondage. (Luke 13:11)
5. At a Pharisee's house eating a meal with the host and several lawyers, Jesus heals a man with dropsy. (Luke 14:2)
6. A man who is disabled and unable to walk is healed at the pool of Bethesda. (John 5:8-9)
7. Jesus heals a man who was born blind at the pool of Siloam. (John 9:14)

My Strength Is Your Strength

MY STRENGTH IS ... _____

45 | ROBBED AT GUNPOINT

On September 23, 1990 at 8:20 p.m. I was robbed. I was in front of my apartment. It was on the corner of Kingshighway & Hooke. My sister and I had our first apartment together. This was our gift from our mother after we graduated from high school. At the point of the robbery however, my sister had already moved out of the apartment because we had quickly learned that we couldn't live together.

I was with my children's father, about to get out the car and a guy with huge lips came from behind the bushes. When I opened the door he said, "B_ _ _ _, if you scream or holler … you are dead." He put the gun in my ear. It was a huge gun. My son Eric was sitting on my lap. He was 11 months old, about to turn one on October 2. The guy pulled me out of the car and jumped in. He put the gun to my son's father's head asking for money and his car. Another guy was with him. He was on the driver's side, outside the car where my son's father was sitting. They got what they wanted without killing us but this left me very paranoid for a very … l o n g time. They even got away with my son's diaper bag, but I am alive to tell about it so that was a blessing.

I was so scared after that experience that we moved out of that apartment and moved to Aurora, Colorado where my children's aunt lived. We didn't stay there long. Only about a year until I felt comfortable enough to move back home. The police did find the car, but they never did find the suspects. As years went by I suspected this was a set up by someone we knew. We had just dropped off my son's father's friend around the corner from our place. It just seemed likely they were waiting for us.

Keep your circle small. Know your surroundings. Follow your gut. Seek counseling after traumatic events. Everyone is not your friend. It is not good when people are jealous of you and they want what you have. You can't trust everybody. If you feel a person is not good for you, don't pressure the relationship.

My Strength Is Your Strength

46 | ERIC AND ANTHONY

Eric is my firstborn child. He was born premature. I was seven months pregnant (27 weeks) when I gave birth to him. I was 17 years old and a senior in high school. Eric was born on Oct 2, at Regional Hospital in St. Louis, MO. I remember calling my mother while she was at work saying, "Mama I feel like I am peeing on myself." She said, "Call your doctor." My doctor told me to go to the emergency room. Eric weighed three pounds one ounce when he was born. Eric was so small. I remember telling the doctors and nurses, "I feel like I am going to break him, he is so small." Eric couldn't come home until he weighed five pounds. He was in the hospital until the day before Thanksgiving, November, 1989. Eric was a pretty good baby … he never cried. My children's grandmother kept Eric while I finished my last year in high school. He would stay with her Monday through Friday. She was a huge blessing. She was looking out for me more than I realized. It takes a village.

Eric's name means "complete ruler." The original form is Erik, which has been borne by nine Danish Kings. It is also used as a nickname for Frederic and Frederick. A notable bearer was Eirkr inn Rauda (Eric the Red),

149

a tenth-century navigator and explorer who discovered Greenland. This was also the name of several early kings of Sweden, Denmark and Norway.

The one thing I can say about both of my children is they never talked back to me. They are polite and have very good manners. They have never been to jail, not to my knowledge anyway. I haven't had to pay bail for either of them. I am very proud of both of them. Neither of them are college graduates. Eric went to college for two years and decided college wasn't for him. Eric was 19 years old when I was first diagnosed with breast cancer. I don't believe college is for everyone. I knew it wasn't for my sons because I saw the gifts and talents in their hands. Eric was a child putting things together without instructions. Anthony knew he didn't want to go to college.

Anthony was 12 years old when I was diagnosed with breast cancer the first time and 14 years old when I was diagnosed the second time. I wanted to live especially for Anthony because he was the youngest of my children. I knew my oldest son would survive because he was already out of my house and away in college but Anthony was still at home, young, and needed me. My heart truly goes out to the children that lose their parents to cancer.

Anthony started cutting his own hair when he was 12 years old. I believe he started cutting his own hair because I was going through cancer and I forgot about his haircuts. Anthony was born on May 19. Anthony

weighed six pounds twelve ounces. He was born at
Deaconess Hospital. I experienced postpartum depression
with him and I believed it had a lot to do with being a
single parent and the realities of life hitting me. I was a
single mother of two before the age of 25 and that is a big
responsibility!

Anthony is an English name. His name means highly
praiseworthy and is derived from a Roman Clan name.
In the seventeenth century, the spelling Anthony was
associated with the Greek Anthos, meaning flower.
Anthony and Eric's favorite color is blue. Anthony
graduated from barber school on his nineteenth birthday.
He is doing well. Some of his clients are childhood
friends. Anthony is walking in purpose and passion. He
loves what he is doing and you can tell.

I always wanted sons but as life continues I wish I
would've had at least one daughter. Be careful what you
pray for and speak out of your mouth.

I love our sons … Eric and Anthony.

My Strength Is Your Strength

MY STRENGTH IS ... _____

47 | LEFTY

Southpaw: Nickname for a left-handed person

We are lefties ... my twin and I. If it wasn't for my late
Aunt Moné, my dad's only sister (who, coincidentally,
was also a breast cancer survivor before the age of 40),
we might have been right-handed too, but she wanted to
make sure we would be lefties. Very seldom is someone
left-handed. In fact only about 10 percent of the world's
population are lefties. Look around and you'll notice ...
most everyone sitting around a table is writing with their
right hand.

As a kid I would often hear people say, "We have a
'soft paw' in the room." At least, that's what I thought
they were saying. It's "SOUTHPAW!" All these years I
thought people were saying "soft paw."

The term "southpaw" originated from the practice in
baseball of arranging the diamond with the batter facing
east to avoid the afternoon sun. A left-handed pitcher
facing west would therefore have his pitching arm
toward the south of the diamond. As the third edition of

"The Dickson Baseball Dictionary" points out, however, that origin story is a little simpler. The earliest baseball mention of a "southpaw" is found by Tom Shieber, senior curator at the National Baseball Hall of Fame. It appeared in the New York Atlas in 1858, but in reference to a left-handed first baseman, not a pitcher. Boston Globe baseball writer and former ballplayer Tim Murnane also recalled in a 1908 edition of Arizona's Bisbee Daily Review that a St. Louis newspaper had called him a "southpaw" in 1875 because he was a left-handed batter. Murnane adopted the term in describing pitchers "simply because they were left -handed, and not because they pitched the ball towards the sunny south on certain grounds.

While the sport of baseball has seen its fair share of southpaw superstars, its most famous left-handed slugger is, without question, the Sultan of Swat (Babe Ruth).

Angelina Jolie, BRCA2 positive, prophylactic double mastectomy is left-handed.

Left-handed women have a higher risk of breast cancer than right-handed women and the effect is greater post-menopausal. (British Journal of Cancer 97, 686- 687. (28 August 2007) L Fritschi, M Divitini, A Talbot- Smith.)

Scientists have long wondered why left-handed people are a rarity. Stories about being slapped on the wrist for being a lefty aside, there must be some deeper, evolutionary reason. Scientists figure, a new study suggests lefties are rare because of the balance between cooperation and competition in human evolution.

Lefties are better able to multi-task. One of the advantages of being left-handed is that it forces your brain to think quicker. The more dominant the left handedness is, the better these abilities are. Some left-handed individuals have better memories.

In his book, *Right-hand, Left Hand*, University College London psychologist Chris McManus states that lefties have made up a disproportionately large number of high achievers throughout history. Perhaps that explains why lefty Supreme Court Justice, Ruth Bader Ginsburg has presided on the nation's highest court for years.

Famous Lefties
Former President Barack Obama and Oprah Winfrey are both left-handed.

Ronald Reagan and Barack Obama have both signed bills into law with their left hands. And being left-handed certainly did not hold back the artistic achievements of Michelangelo or Raphael.

Paul McCartney took up the bass guitar as a child, however he found it difficult to play right-handed so he reversed the strings and the rest is history. He now plays a true left-handed bass. Paul McCartney also shares the same birthday as my twin and I … June 18.

When pop star Lady Gaga sings about being "Born This Way" she could very well be talking about being left handed.

British chef Gordon Ramsey is a lefty, and judging from all of his Michelin stars, that dominant left hand may just give him an upper hand in the kitchen.

Judy Garland, renowned singer and actress was left-handed, leaving moviegoers everywhere with the impression that, "There's no place like home," and no star like a lefty.

In his book, *The Puzzle of Left-Handedness*, author Rik Smits presents the theory that lefties derive from identical twins. Wow!!!! More specifically, because identical twins have mirror traits, Smits pontificates that lefties are the result of these embryos splitting in the womb.

Perhaps that explains why Mary-Kate Olsen is a lefty and her sister, Ashley, is a righty. Whatever the reason, though, it's the perfect arrangement for signing autographs next to your twin.

A famous list of lefty's: Whoopi Goldberg, Nicole Kidman, Julia Roberts, Adam Levine, Morgan Freeman, Prince William, Jennifer Lawrence, Celine Dion (a two-time breast cancer survivor, I might add), Tom Cruise, Eminem, Keanu Reeves, Tina Fey, Steve Jobs, Bill Gates, Albert Einstein, Benjamin Franklin, Issac

Newton, Justin Bieber, Will Ferrell, Sarah Jessica Parker, Matthew Broderick, Caitlyn Jenner, Jerry Seinfield, Jason Alexander, Trey Parker, Jason Sudeikis, Ben Stiller, Seth Rogen and Tim Allen are ALL left-handed.

I am a proud left-hander. #Winning

My Strength Is Your Strength

MY STRENGTH IS ... _____

48 | PEARLS

I literally wear pearls every day, well almost every day.
Sometimes I will put my diamonds on. I have given away
an estimated 3,000 pairs of earrings in the past three
years to girls and women all over the country and around
the world. This is my way of giving back and reminding
women they are beautiful regardless of what might come
their way. While I was going through breast cancer and
even the aftermath of breast cancer, I rarely felt like
dressing up, but pearls dressed me up.

Pearls make any outfit look good.

Every woman should have pearls. Every girl should be
introduced to pearls. Pearls should be a part of a woman's
wardrobe. Pearls can be expensive or inexpensive it all
depends on you and your bank account.

A pearl is said to symbolize the purity, generosity,
integrity, and loyalty of the wearer. Diamonds may be a
girl's best friend but, for me, I prefer pearls!!!

My Strength Is Your Strength

**MY STRENGTH IS ...** _____

49 | VALEDA'S HOPE

I knew I wanted to give back after going through breast cancer and surviving it. I also realized I wanted to give recliners to women that undergo a double mastectomy due the diagnosis of breast cancer. I didn't know how I was going to do this but I knew I wanted to. I was pretty young when I was dealing with breast cancer and I would attend events related to breast cancer and I realized I didn't see anyone my own age. I wanted my peers to know that breast cancer is real and it happens to the best of us. I gave my first breast cancer awareness conference in November, 2012. I paid for it with my own money. I purchased the first recliner with my own money. It was suggested to me to become a not-for-profit organization for funding and sponsorships. And so it was … Valeda's Hope was born out of a dream and officially became a 501(c)(3) NFP organization on April 11, 2013.

Our Vision: To navigate women through the breast cancer process from mammogram to survivorship and to educate women on health issues.

Our Mission Statement: To win lives by increasing awareness of breast cancer through education and early detection and to provide mammograms for those in need. We also provide the following nurturing services: massages, manicures, physical therapy, emotional therapy and genetic testing.

Valeda's Hope Programs:

Recliners For Her

We deliver recliners to women that have been diagnosed with breast cancer and will undergo a double mastectomy. We will also give a recliner to women who have prophylactic surgery due to the BRCA2 gene. Most of Valeda's Hope's recliners are delivered in Missouri and Illinois but Valeda's Hope has driven as far away as Michigan to deliver a recliner. And certainly the farthest delivery was when Valeda's Hope purchased a recliner for the Phambilli community in South Africa.

Comfort Items For Her

Every woman undergoing a double mastectomy or prophylactic surgery receives a blanket, a pillow, magazines, cards of encouragement, back scratchers, and soft peppermints to help soothe them as they recover from surgery.

Girlz Fit Night/Nordstrom

Women and teenagers come together to network and buy professionally fit, pretty new bras and but more importantly to become more aware about breast cancer and the importance of self-breast exams and regular mammograms.

Valeda's Hope Pink & Pearls Luncheon
Our biggest fundraiser! Women come out in their pink and pearls ... men wear their pink shirts and ties! This luncheon is where we serve the community, honor the survivors, hear about the latest research and treatment options from top breast-care physicians, and surgeons, support local vendors, and raise funds to continue winning lives. Valeda's Hope Pink & Pearls Luncheon is every third Saturday in October from Noon to 3 p.m. and includes some great entertainment as well. We've had dancers, singers, poetry readers, artists, comedians and authors. Since 2012, it has grown from 75 winning women to 220 winning women. I personally funded the first conference but now it has grown into our biggest fundraising event of the year with the hopes of each year topping the year before.

Valeda's Hope Mobile Mammogram Day
We have two mobile mammogram days a year at the St. Ann Public Library. Our event is held on a Saturday in June and December — our target months. We serve a light snack and distribute brochures on women's health, breast cancer awareness, and upcoming events. We collaborate with Siteman Cancer Center and Mercy Breast Center for the use of their mammogram van. (Valeda's Hope Mammogram Van Coming Soon).

The purpose is to serve the 9-5 working woman and the under-insured woman by providing affordable mammograms.

Mammogram Monday
Valeda's Hope promotes the importance of regular mammograms every Monday on social media via Facebook, Instagram, Twitter, and LinkedIn. This is done faithfully every week for 52 weeks every year. Visit us at www.valedashope.org.

Accomplishments & Impact
- 2012 – Valeda's Hope was founded
- 2012 – Interviewed by Vickie Newton, Emmy award-winning journalist and founder of the online magazine, *TheVillageCelebration.com*
- 2013 – I received the New Balance® Survivor of the Year Award, where I received New Balance Lace Up For The Cure Collection® and recognition at the Susan G. Komen Race. While training for the Susan G. Komen 5k race, I was healing and wearing a wound vac machine from an infection after surgery #6.
- 2013 – My family and I were featured in the *St. Louis Post-Dispatch* newspaper for being carriers of the gene mutation BRCA2, after Angelina Jolie went public about her prophylactic double mastectomy due to the same gene mutation.
- 2013 – Selected as a guest writer for Susan G. Komen Blog (St. Louis Affiliate)

- 2013 – Featured In The St. Louis Rams *Insider Magazine*
- 2013 – Featured on Billboards for YMCA Livestrong Exercise Program For Survivors
- 2013 – Featured on Channel 5 with my twin, Vanessa for the Susan G. Komen Race
- 2014 – Graduated from PEcad CoHort
- October 2015 and October 2016 — Expanded the Pink & Pearls Luncheon to Flint, Michigan
- October 2015 – Featured and contributing writer for *Redbook Magazine*
- October 2015 – Featured and contributing writer for *Heart & Soul Magazine*
- 2016 – Guest Speaker at Hawthorn Leadership School For Girls
- 2016 – Fox2Now featured me and my husband delivering a recliner to a double mastectomy client.
- 2016 – Health Panelist for Sigma Gamma Rho Annual Conference in St. Louis, MO
- 2016 – Valeda's Hope moved from her basement to a new office building in Brentwood, MO
- 2017 – Purchased a recliner for the Phambilii Community in Capetown, South Africa
- 2017 – Valeda Keys spoke at the largest AIDS Centre in Durban, South African
- 2018 – Contributing writer for Community News Publications
- 2019 – Received proclamation from the City of St. Louis Mayor, Lyda Krewson (I have my own day for the works of Valeda's Hope, March 27, 2019.)

- April 2019 — Voted Councilwoman at the Municpal Election, Ward 4
- May 2019 — Received The Woman Of Achievement Award (Health Advocacy) for my volunteer efforts, and demonstrating dedication and commitment to improving the quality of life in the St. Louis community. The St. Louis Women Of Achievement Award is the oldest, ongoing program in the area with the sole mission to honor and recognize the volunteer efforts of women. It was established in 1933. I am forever grateful for this acknowledgement.

I also regularly speak at churches, workshops, seminars and schools.

My Strength Is Your Strength

50 | BLACK WOMEN AND BREAST CANCER

Black women are two to three times more likely than white women to get an aggressive type of breast cancer called triple negative. White women in the U.S. are slightly more likely to develop breast cancer than black women but less likely to die of it. Black women are the ones that are more likely to die from breast cancer for many reasons. Some of those reasons include: the cancer or tumor is found late, there may be a lack of resources both financially and educationally, and there may be differences in health insurance or lack of insurance all together.

St. Louis is number two in the U.S. for women dying of breast cancer at an alarming rate.

The good news is, research has improved breast cancer treatments and survival rates over the years and every day there are new studies and new findings to further breast cancer survival rates in black women.

My Strength Is Your Strength

MY STRENGTH IS ... _____

51 | CHEMOTHERAPY

I always get the question, "Did you have to have chemo?" I think that question is asked because my hair is long and healthy. Chemotherapy was never a treatment option for me. Thank God. What is chemotherapy? Chemotherapy is a treatment option that uses drugs to stop the growth of cancer cells. Chemotherapy may be given by mouth, injection, infusion, or on the skin, depending on the type and stage of the cancer being treated. Some of the side effects are hair loss, neuropathy, weight gain or weight loss, nausea and vomiting, nail beds turning blue, loss of appetite, low red blood cell count and anemia, tiredness, anxiety and depression. Both my mother and my aunt had chemotherapy. A port-a-cath is an implantable port. It is a thin, soft, flexible plastic tube that goes into the vein. It has a port, or opening, just under the skin of the chest or arm. The port has a thin rubber disc which special needles can pass medicines into, or take blood from. I heard that the port placement was painful from one of Valeda's Hope clients but I don't have any personal experience with a port-a-cath since I personally did not have to get one.

My Strength Is Your Strength

MY STRENGTH IS ... _____

52 | HIS POINT OF VIEW

I would advise any wife or anyone that's in a serious relationship to sit down and have that conversation with your mate. Ask him or her questions. Do not be afraid to ask, "What you feel in your heart." It is better to know than not know. My husband was very supportive and was present at all seven surgeries. If your mate is not supportive while you are going through breast cancer or anything else that is vitally important to the other person, please evaluate the relationship. Here are some of the questions and answers I asked and received from my husband.

1. What would you say to a man after his wife has been diagnosed with breast cancer? Pray and be supportive.
2. How do you continue to be intimate with your wife after she loses her breasts? It doesn't change the person, it just changes some things. For example, my husband said it never made a difference with me cleaning the house. Ha Ha!! My husband cleans everything and I do mean everything. You can eat off our garage floor. Bring some humor in where you can.

3. How are you available to her emotionally? By listening and being attentive.
4. Is it okay for a man to cry with his wife? Yes, if he has some tears.
5. What do you do the day of surgery? Be There!
6. Did you want to leave or do you want to leave? No, you would have to be a heartless person.
7. Would you still be attracted to me if I didn't have the reconstruction surgery? Yes, if it was me I would have just had them removed and be done with it.
8. What do you think about my "new breasts"? They don't move!
9. Who is your support while I go through this? God, who else is it going to be?
10. Did your job know or assist with my breast cancer challenge? What are they going to do? They gave me days off when you had your surgeries.
11. Did you talk about it to anyone? Not really.

I would recommend you ask your spouse or your partner similar questions that are suitable for where you are in your relationship.

My Strength Is Your Strength

53 | OPPORTUNITY OF A LIFETIME

In 2015 I was asked to go to South Africa by a woman
named Mrs. Burton, who is a board member of the Zonta
Club. I first met her after I was featured in Redbook
magazine. She wanted a copy of the magazine to take to
the Zonta Club Board of Directors, from whom Valeda's
Hope was seeking funding. After our first meeting she
asked me to go to Africa with her. I was so honored
but, at the time, I just couldn't see my way clear to go.
I was in the middle of planning my annual Valeda's Hope
conference amongst a multitude of other things. Regrettably,
I had to decline because I had too much on my plate.

Over the course of the next year I kept in touch with Mrs.
Burton because I was so impressed with her strength and
her style. Mrs. Burton and her husband have built two
churches in South Africa – Bethesda Evangelical Church
and South African Evangelistic Mission. I learned that
Mrs. Burton's husband died about seven years ago, yet
Mrs. Burton is still carrying on their legacy in South Africa.

In 2016, Mrs. Burton asked me again about going on a
trip to South Africa with her. I was still very busy with

work, Valeda's Hope and life in general so once again I had to decline.

Finally, November 2017, we made it happen!! I didn't want to say "no" again. We went to Cape Town and Durban, South Africa together! It took us 22 hours to get there but it was worth it! We got to spend three weeks there. I spoke at two churches – including one of the churches that Mr. and Mrs. Burton had built and I also had the privilege of speaking at an AIDS center.

Before I departed St. Louis, my mother gave me a journal to keep while in Africa. That journal was the best thing ever while I was there. It was the ideal way for me to record my trip but, more importantly, it was a special place to capture the true essence of my trip – the emotions, the smells, the teachings, the learnings, the food, the people, the customs, the blessings.

Sometimes you need others to think for you especially when they believe in you. Even though Mrs. Burton was my mentor, I learned that mentors learn from their mentees as well. While on our trip, Mrs. Burton taught me things and, at the same time, I taught her things.

The day we left for Africa I was very nervous, slightly depressed, concerned about the length of the flight, and feeling overweight. We were flying on South African Airways, operated by United Airlines in economy seats. I couldn't help but wonder how this was all going to work out. I had never traveled to another continent. I didn't know exactly what to expect. I was even worried about things like bowel movements and if I might have a panic attack. Although, at one point, I did have a panic attack, my concerns quickly turned to gratitude. I sat next to a man from Germany. He was a retired teacher ... traveling alone ... to see the world. He told me his wife died of cancer a year ago. He had dreamed to see the Arch, the Missouri History Museum and Forest Park in St. Louis. I was so impressed with him because it was just him and his map. How brave of him!!!! One thing he said to me was, "When a spouse dies, life must go on whether you like it or not." Wow!!! He was traveling from St. Louis to New York and then Washington D.C. next. His story had a powerful impact on my story and helped give me calm in a moment of my own panic.

Something very special happened while I was in South Africa. I was able to live out the mission of Valeda's Hope by purchasing a recliner for The Phambili Community. The recliner will be for women diagnosed with breast cancer and who must undergo a double mastectomy. Unlike in the USA, these ladies will have to share the recliner and take good care of it after each use since there is only one recliner for them to pass around. But they were so thankful and grateful for our donation and I had the privilege of planting the seed of Valeda's Hope in a special place with some amazing women a long, long, long way from home.

I was also able to give out over 200 sets of pearl earrings which has become my "Valeda's Hope signature," although I wish I would have had more of the small pearl earrings for more of the little girls. And for the children, I gave them pencils. Pencils in America are such a basic item, but in South Africa they are a treasure.

Did you know that December 1st is World AIDS Day? I got tested for AIDS in one of the church's Mrs. Burton and her husband built at a clinic inside the church. My test results were negative. I was told that the people in South Africa are more ashamed of Tuberculosis than HIV. Also inside the church built by the Burton's is a dentist's office. The health clinic and the dentist office help provide much needed health care to the poor and under served from all around the area.

In fact, on December 5, 2017, while I was at the clinic I met a woman who had recently found out she had breast cancer. She was 73 years old and a Muslim. She hadn't told her family yet. A group of us prayed together for her before we left that day. Since I've been home, I often wonder how she is doing. I met a lot of amazing women and men while in Africa. They were warm, welcoming, brave and strong. I now consider myself to have more brothers and sisters, nieces and nephews than I did before I went to South Africa.

I was in Africa for 21 days and I learned so much. One of the first things that Mrs. Burton taught me was that if a woman doesn't know her style she is in bad shape. Mrs. Burton is definitely a lady who knows her style and she complimented me daily on my style. I also learned that sometimes it's better to speak less rather than more, because sometimes people are trying to decide if you are from where they are from. I realized while I was traveling that a lot of people had never heard of St. Louis. I learned very quickly that our US dollar is so much stronger than the African rand. In fact, when I was in Africa our dollar was worth about 13 times what the rand was worth. I learned that, despite what you might think, it is very expensive to live in Africa and that not everyone in Africa is poor. I learned that a Chevrolet Cruze is considered a luxury car and you have to be 18 years old to get a driver's license which is the same age you can drink alcohol. When you live in South Africa you retire at the age of 60 and because of a perpetual water shortage you can't shower more than two minutes in Cape Town or you will get fined. I learned that Americans are blessed to have so many great stores that make our lives so much easier including my favorite, the The Dollar Store! In South Africa people have far less access to daily necessities, they have to travel long distances and go to multiple stores to get everything they need. Life in South Africa is more simple and yet more complicated at the same time. I learned a few words while I was in Cape Town such as: Hooe gaan dit = How are you?, Lekker slap = Good night, and my personal favorite ... Eish = Wow!!!

A powerful part of my trip was our visit to Robben Island. This is where Nelson Mandela spent 18 years of his 27 years in prison. This is a must visit. It takes about three hours for the complete tour. The ferry ride to the island takes about thirty minutes. Our tour guide was an ex-convict which was very insightful. He was able to show us Nelson Mandela's actual prison cell. This was pretty emotional.

We also met Christo Brand. He was a former Robben Island warden and the author of *Doing Life With Mandela, My Prisoner, My Friend*. I would definitely like to visit Robben Island again. People come from all over the world to see Robben Island. Some of the other places I visited while I was in Cape Town were: Bo-Kaap Museum, Kirstenbosch Gardens, a National Botanical Garden well-known all over the world and a must-see, Table Mountain (1,085m), where you are in a cable car that holds 67 people ... if you're afraid of heights this wouldn't be for you, you must wear a jacket or long sleeves because it gets colder once you reach the top and you can take photos, buy souvenirs and eat in the café. I would also recommend visiting Camp's Bay and Victoria and Alfred Waterfront. We didn't get a chance to eat at Gold Restaurant but we were able to grab dessert at Tasha's. We had carrot cake and ice cream. Mrs. Burton had coffee with her cake.

**Winning Tips For International Travel and Good
Stuff Not to Forget:**

1. Travel with an empty water bottle – water is
   expensive. You can easily fill your water bottle up at
   water fountains.
2. Download WhatsApp – You can talk to your family
   and friends for free.
3. Wireless charger/universal adapter
4. Small personal fan
5. Scarf – the weather is always changing and your neck
   should be protected to help keep you comfortable.
6. Wear comfortable shoes and clothing with a hood
   while traveling for a long period of time just in case
   it starts raining.
7. Small umbrella
8. Ear plugs
9. Contact your mobile phone service for international
   rates prior to departure trip.
10. Dress in layers or bring a cardigan while on the
    airplane. Sometimes it's cold on the airplane.
11. Pack your medicine in your carry-on bag. Ask
    your doctor for anti-anxiety medication if you have
    anxiety.
12. Hand sanitizer and hand lotion
13. "Thank you" takes you places your degree won't.
    Learn the word thank you in different languages.
    Dankie = "Thank You" in Cape Town, South Africa.
14. Watch the foods you eat. Eat mostly fruits and
    vegetables to prevent bloating.
15. Use your credit card for most purchases.
16. Convert your dollars to the local currency.

17. Check your flight 24 hours in advance.
18. Weigh your luggage before leaving on your trip. The cost of extra weight can be costly.
19. Wear the same outfits with different accessories.
20. Pray that your luggage is safe.
21. Recline your seat and let down your armrest while you're flying.
22. Use the lockbox at your hotel. Put in a code that's easy to remember.
23. **ALWAYS PROTECT YOUR PASSPORT!**
24. Make physical copies of your passport and keep them in several different spots in your baggage. Always have a copy with you!
25. Pack travel size Vaseline. You can't go wrong with Vaseline.
26. Travel while you are young … you take more calculated risks when you are younger.
27. Plan your trips at the beginning of the year and start saving.
28. Buy international stamps to mail family and friends postcards.
29. Keep your phone on airplane mode when there is no WiFi.
30. Pack socks in your carry on. You may want to take off your shoes while flying.
31. Hide your makeup in a special place in your suitcase.
32. Feminine wipes
33. Check weather forecast daily
34. Use Uber for transportation, it's much cheaper than a the taxi cab.
35. Give your flight number and itinerary to your family and friends.

36. Take Malaria medication as prescribed.
37. Get up and move around while on long flights to get some exercise and help prevent blood clots.
38. And finally, drink lots and lots of water. It's good for you plus good hydration helps prevent jet lag.

There are many languages and dialects spoken in Africa. It is safer to have an interpreter and host while traveling internationally. If it wasn't for our hosts in South Africa I don't know what we would have done ... Wow!!! OMG!!! Eish!!! Thank you so much!!!

While in South Africa, Mrs. Burton and I did have a misunderstanding and she said to me, "We will have our misunderstandings ... you either get bitter or better, people major on the minor and forget about the higher goal." This was so profound to me. I believe so many awesome relationships have ended because of the MINOR, when the goal should have been the MAJOR.

While in Cape Town, South Africa you're surrounded by the Atlantic Ocean. While In Durban, South Africa you are surrounded by the Indian Ocean. Never in a million years I would've thought I'd experience this. Having breast cancer has done me plenty of favors. Valeda's Hope goes GLOBAL. Both oceans are beautiful. One thing I know for sure that people are the same everywhere, they know when you notice them, they know when their peace is being interrupted, they know when you are beautiful. Everyone wants to be appreciated not

abused or used. Everyone wants to be loved.

I wore the same underwear while in South Africa.
I wash the same underwear nightly. I did this to
decrease. I wanted to see how I could do without all
the convenience. It was definitely humbling. Once Mrs.
Burton figured out what I was doing, she showed me how
to wash out my pajamas and get them dried quickly. You
wash your pajamas and then you roll everything up in a
towel very tight, so the towel catches all the water. She
said, "I know your mother taught you that." I said, "No
she didn't." I never had to wash any of my clothes out
as a kid. We always had a washer and dryer. This was
a reminder to spend more time with my mother and be
grateful for her.

Mrs. Burton also sleeps in one spot. We stayed in 4
different places while in South Africa. She sleeps in one
spot. I sleep all over the bed. As a kid, I never had to
share a bed with my siblings. Even though I was afraid at
night, me and my twin would still end up sleeping with
each other.

South Africa is known for the food and wine. It is
often referred to as The Motherland because "the very
birthplace of the human race." There are 54 independent
countries in Africa and the continent is home to roughly 1
billion people. Nigeria has the largest population.
There is a flower called Protea, it is so beautiful. I also
learned about this while in South Africa. That's why
it's so important to travel. To travel is to learn. Protea is

the name of a genus of South African flowering plants, sometimes called sugarbushes. In local tradition, the Protea flower represents change and hope.

It was an honor to me see Nelson Mandela's face on all the money. I learned so much about him. He had to marry a woman of intellect, sought the sweetness of his mother, he wanted someone that had her strength and resilience. He desired a woman with a strong sense of herself as an individual. He lost interest in one woman because she lacked this. Nelson Mandela truly loved his wife, Winnie Mandela. He was astonished with her stoicism and courage in the face of difficulties. Do you know who you are? Who are you when you are faced with difficulties?

Winnie was a lonely woman and others feared befriending her because of the regular raids on her home and the often visible police presence watching the movements of her and her visitors.

Africa has the highest HIV rate in the world. Hillcrest is the largest town with HIV/AIDS. It was such a honor to go to Hillcrest AIDS Centre Trust to tell my story and give hope. I also gave pearls and pencils out. I reminded them to not put too much pity in the party. Take one second at a time. A diagnosis is just a diagnosis, deal with it accordingly. This was huge for the employees of the AIDS centre because they all had just received some disappointing news about their bonus. Giving them pearls made their day a little special. I heard one employee say

"I got pearls from the USA." It was just ten days until
Christmas. My new sister, Regina had arranged our visit.
Hillcrest AIDS Centre Trust serves several poverty-torn
communities in the Valley of 1000 Hills region – one
of the epicenters of the world's HIV pandemic with
estimated HIV infection rates of up to 40-60 percent of
the population in some communities. The staff are HIV
positive but they work to continue to take care of their
families. There is a 24-bed respite unit for advanced
terminal AIDS (bedridden with no caregiver at home).
We were able to see the bedridden patients and they were
excited to get a "hello." This was a reminder to visit the
sick.

The weather in South Africa while I was there was
around 70 degrees daily. It rained while I was there. It
doesn't snow in South Africa. That's why it's always
good to carry a jacket when traveling. It's summer in
December in Cape Town, South Africa.

One of the main things I wanted to do was go on a Safari.
We were able to go on a Safari while in Durban. It was a
sight to see. I saw so many lions but the elephants stayed
in. Because it was too warm, they were hanging out
under the shade of trees.

Overall, my visit to South Africa was an incredible
experience, very educational and so uplifting.

My Strength Is Your Strength

CONCLUSION

My experience has taught me that life is good, or at least the good outweighs the bad.

Breast cancer is a stumbling block for many. Some have lost the fight, some have won. There are so many things in this life we may want, but just can't have. Don't just take one day at a time, but take one second at a time. Tell your story. It has been a good way of healing from a traumatic experience.

Help others when you can. It may be you in those same shoes one day. Don't put too much pity in the party. Exercise. Drink lots of water. Seek advice. Travel when you can. Take naps. Love your spouse. Love your friends. Love your family. Love what you do for a living. Follow your passion. Be quiet. Forgive quickly. Thank the people who help you. Pray constantly. Laugh when it's funny. Cry when necessary.

I have been dealt some difficult cards, but breast cancer didn't win – I did. I will continue to help other women win where I can and let God and His earthly angels assist me in this earthly realm.

Love & Light,

WORKS CITED

"6 Signs You Have an Infected Wound." *Advanced Tissue*, 28 Aug. 2015, advancedtissue. com/2015/08/6-signs-you-have-an-infected-wound. Accessed 9 Jan. 2019.

"Breast Cancer Stages." *National Breast Cancer Foundation, Inc.*, www.nationalbreastcancer.org/breast-cancer-stages. Accessed 9 Jan. 2019.

"Cytology." *Gale Encyclopedia of Cancer.* Encyclopedia.com, 9 Jan. 2019, www.encyclopedia.com. Accessed 9 Jan. 2019.

Halls. *Moose & Doc Breast Cancer*, 9 Jan. 2019, breast-cancer.ca/?s=comedo+necrosis. Accessed 9 Jan. 2019.

"Ductal carcinoma in situ (DCIS)." *Mayo Clinic*, 16 June 2018, www.mayoclinic.org/ diseases-conditions/dcis/symptoms-causes/syc-20371889. Accessed 9 Jan. 2019.

"Tissue Expanders." *Breast Center, John Hopkins Medicine*, hopkinsmedicine.org/breast_ center/treatments_services/reconstructive_breast_surgery/tissue_expanders.html. Accessed 9 Jan. 2019.

"What is the Women's Health and Cancer Rights Act?" *Find Law*, https://healthcare. findlaw.com/patient-rights/womens-health-and-cancer-rights-act-overview.html. Accessed 9 Jan. 2019.

Made in the
USA
Lexington, KY